I0443301

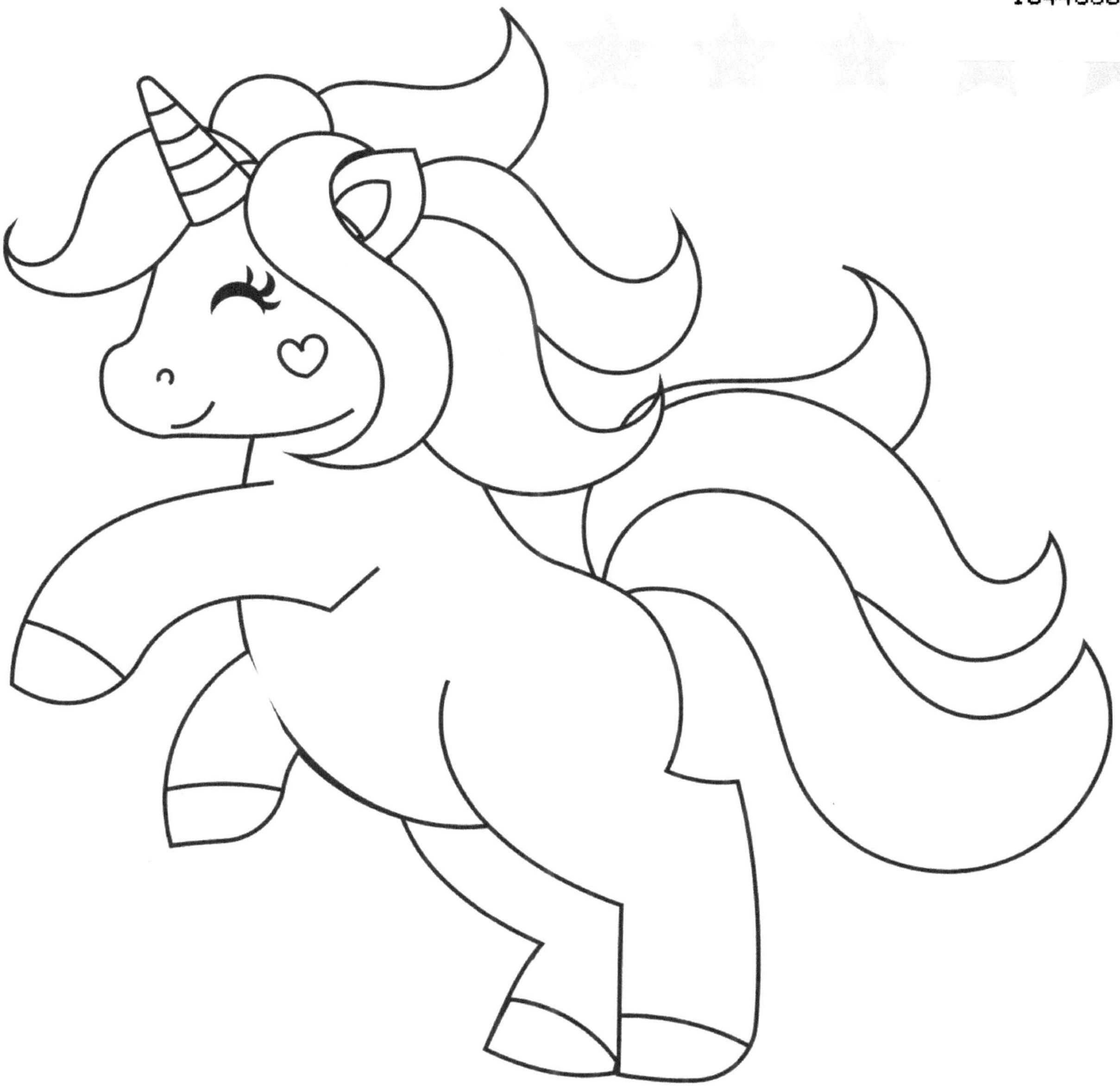

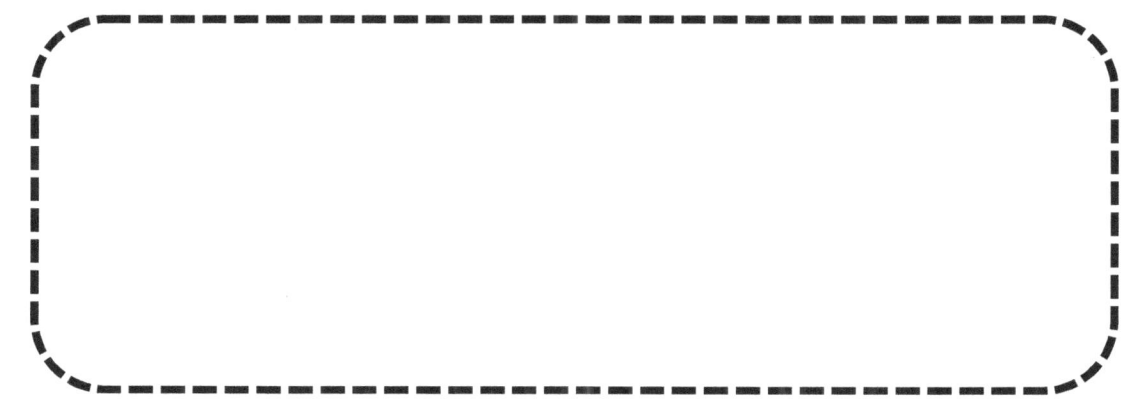

Fantastic!

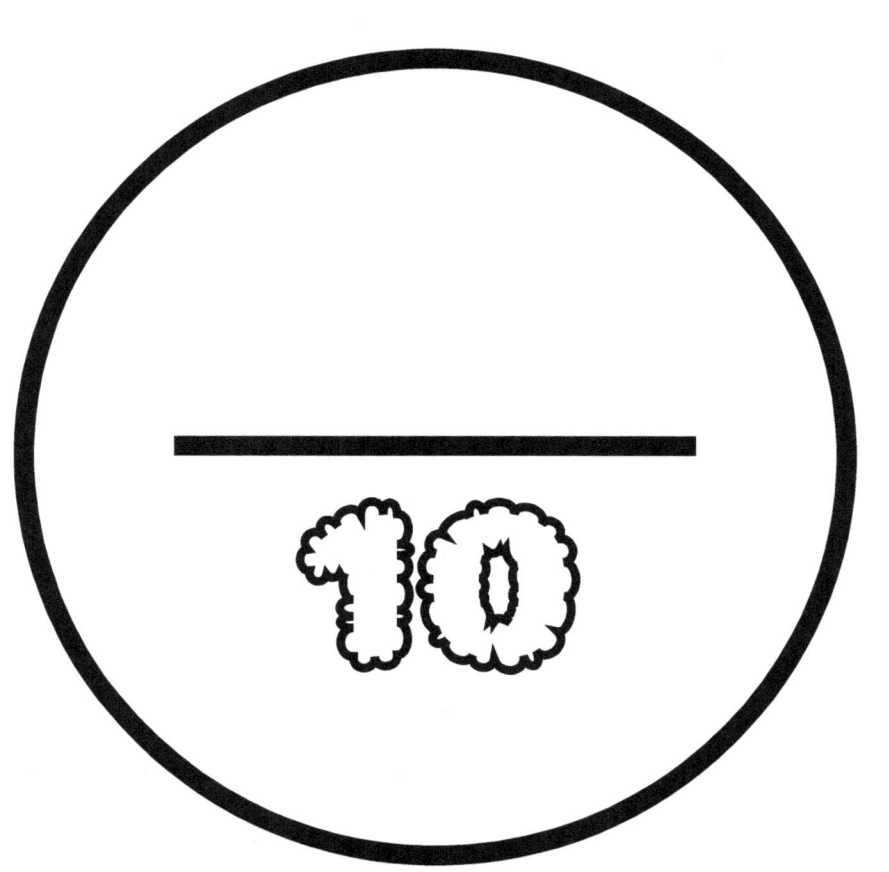

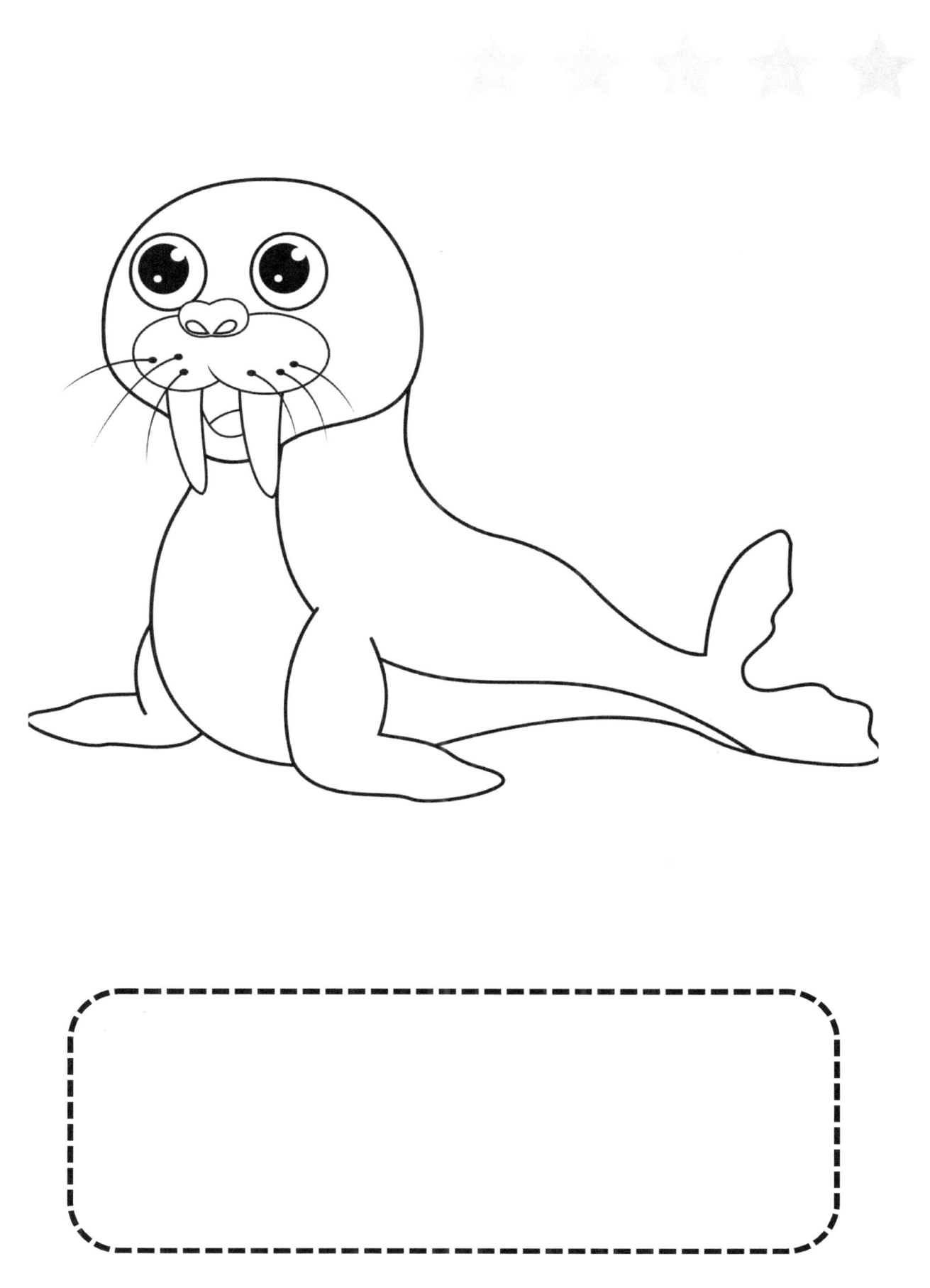

Well done!

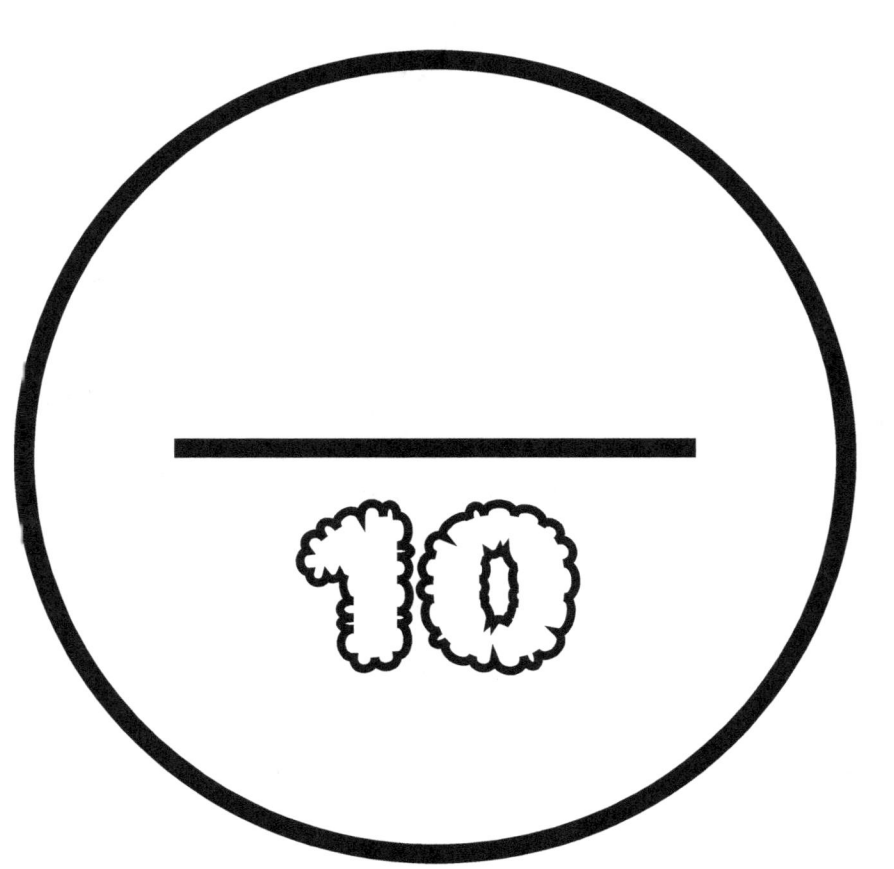

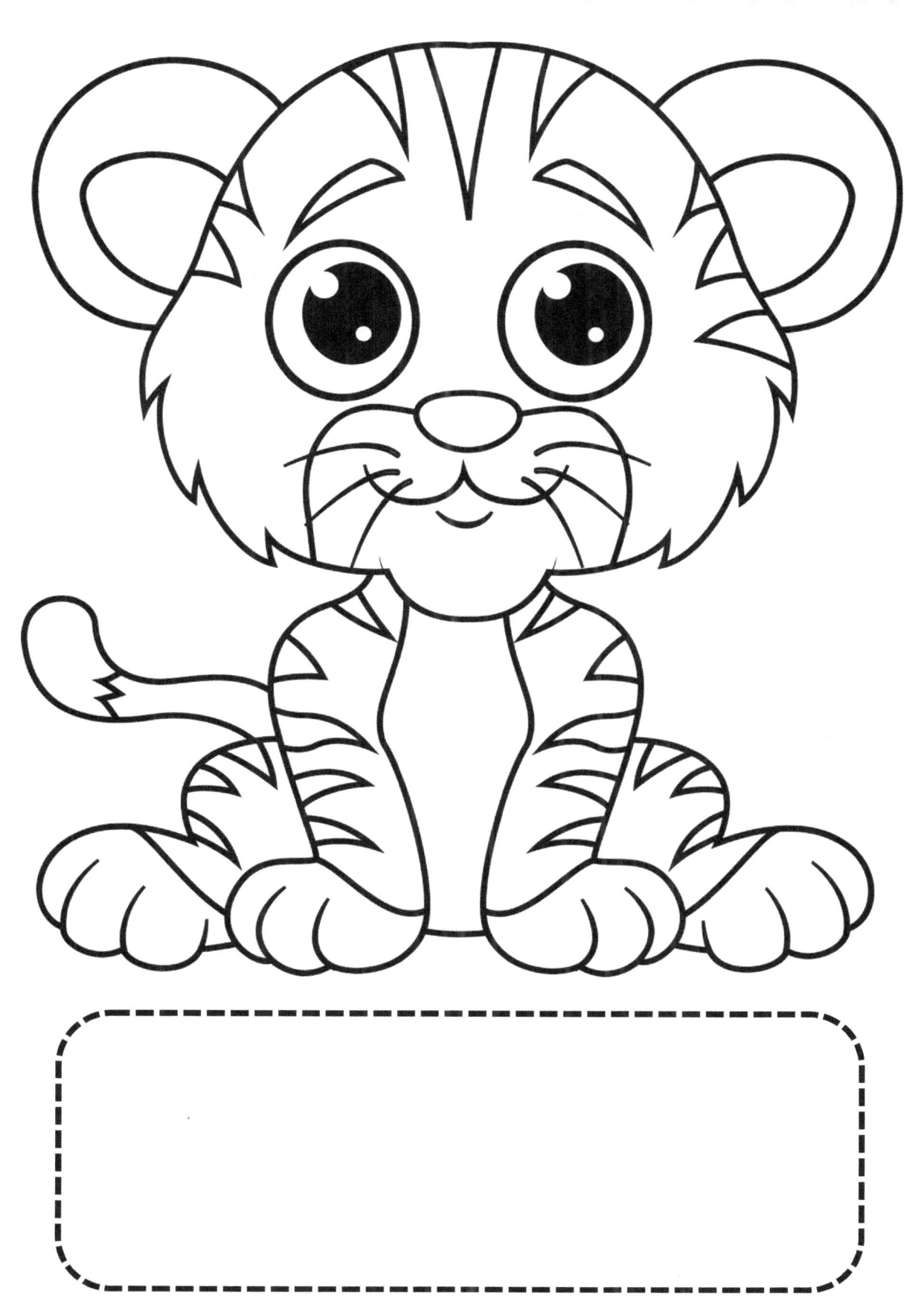

Amazing job!

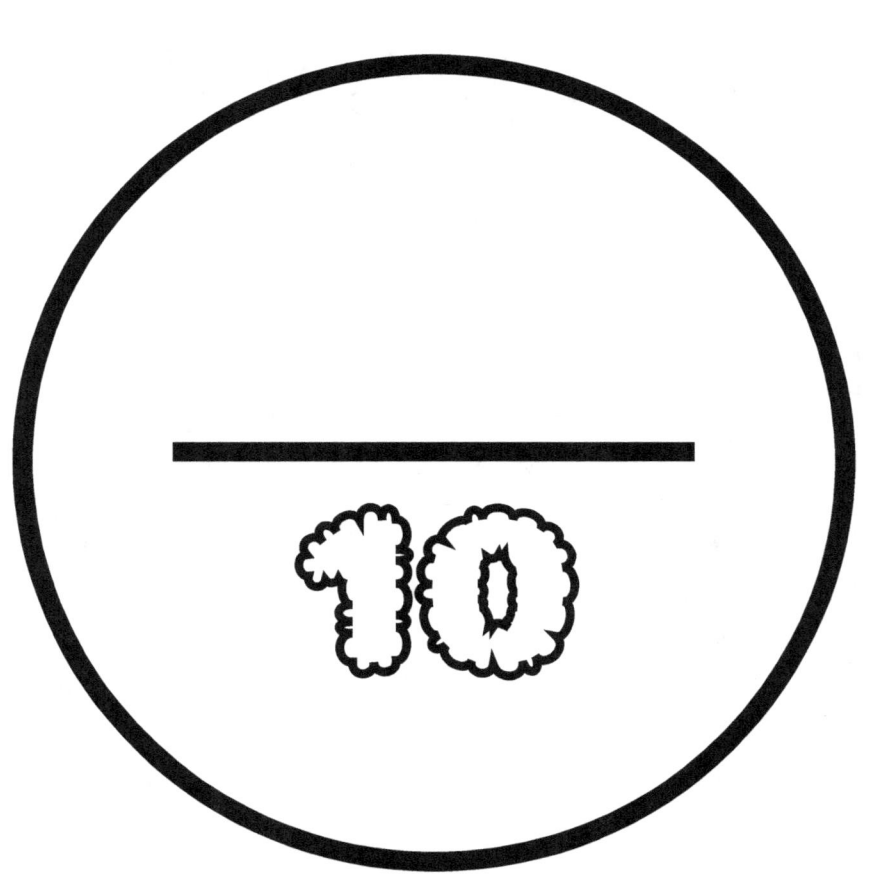

___ / 10

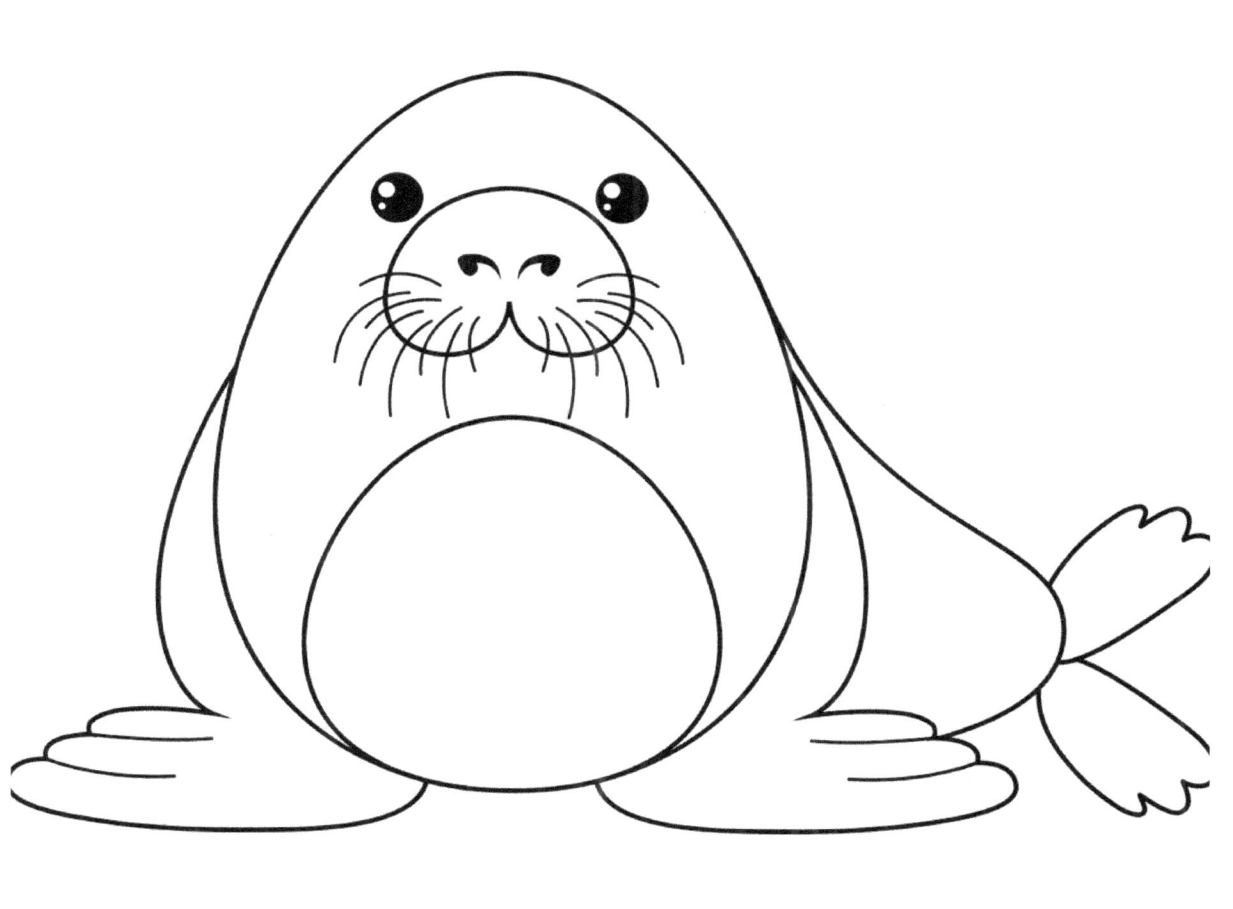
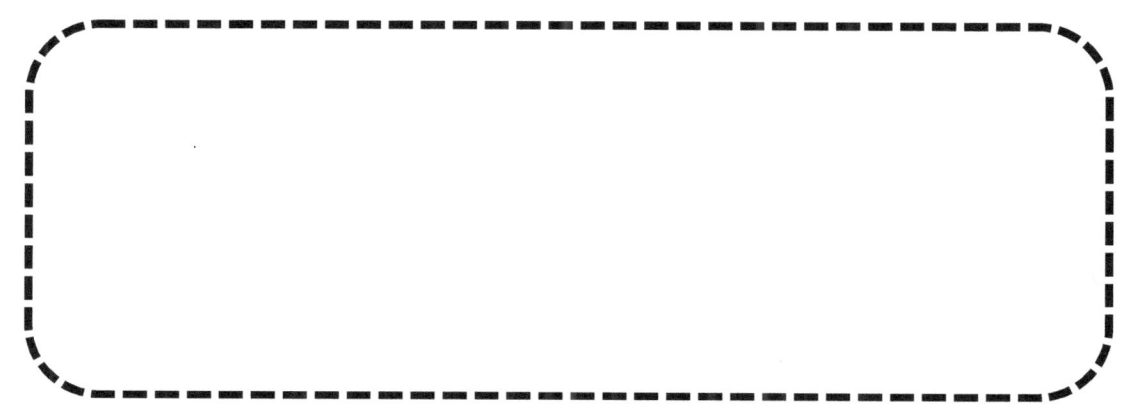

Outstanding!

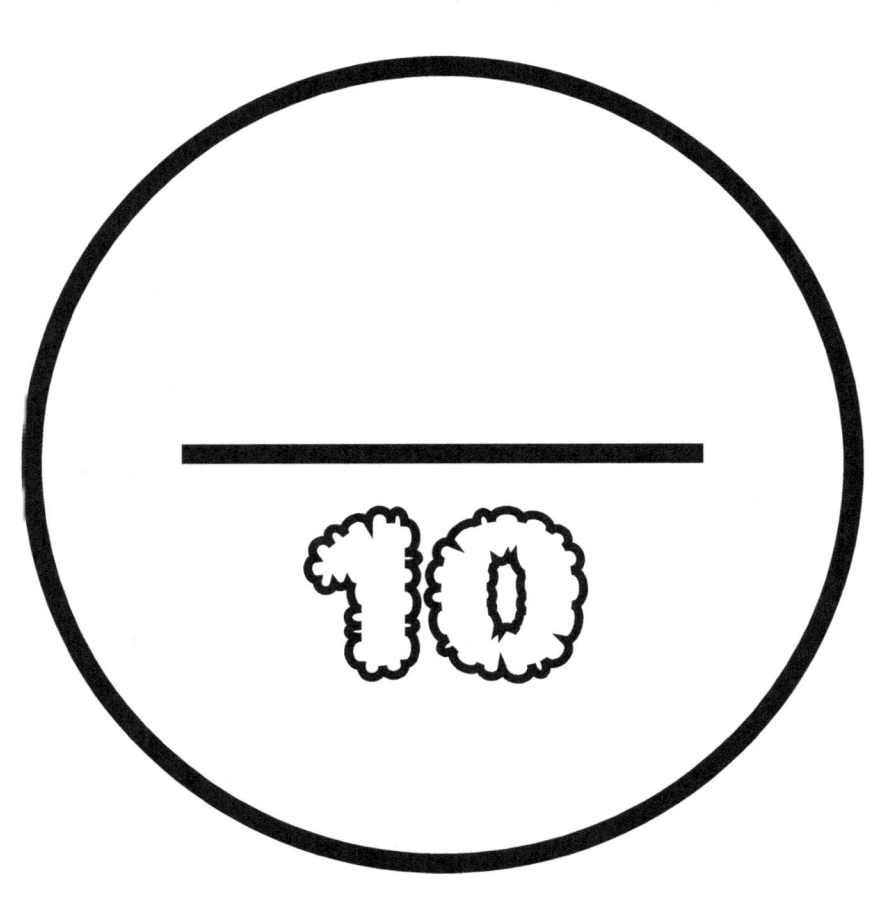

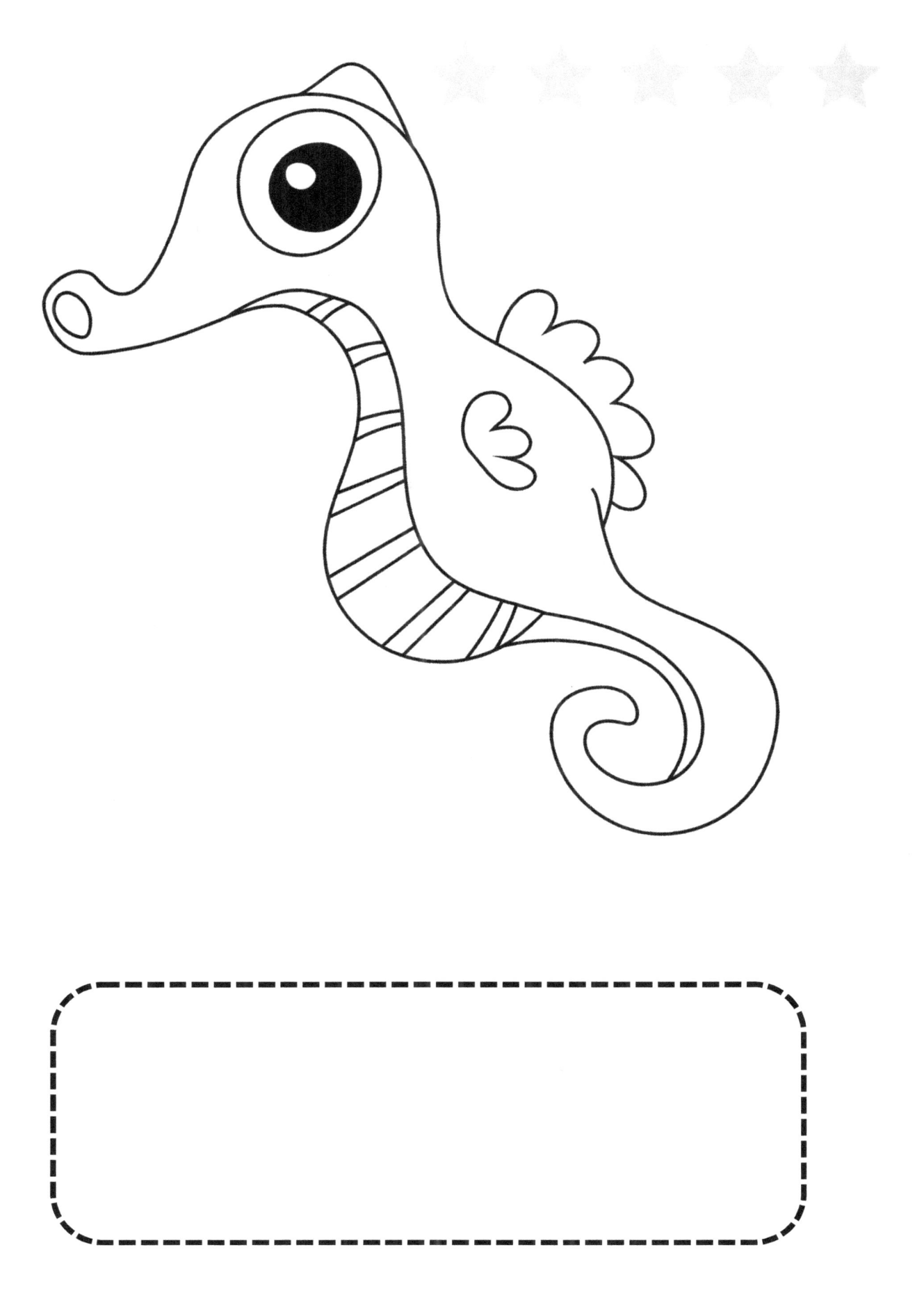

Bravo!

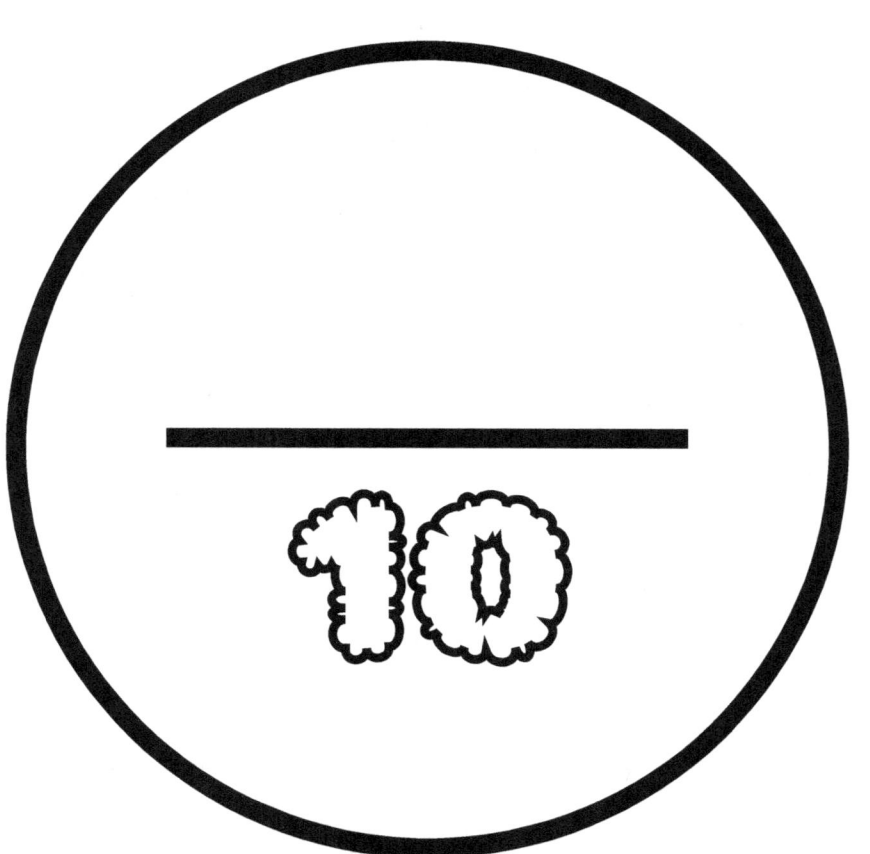

__ / 10

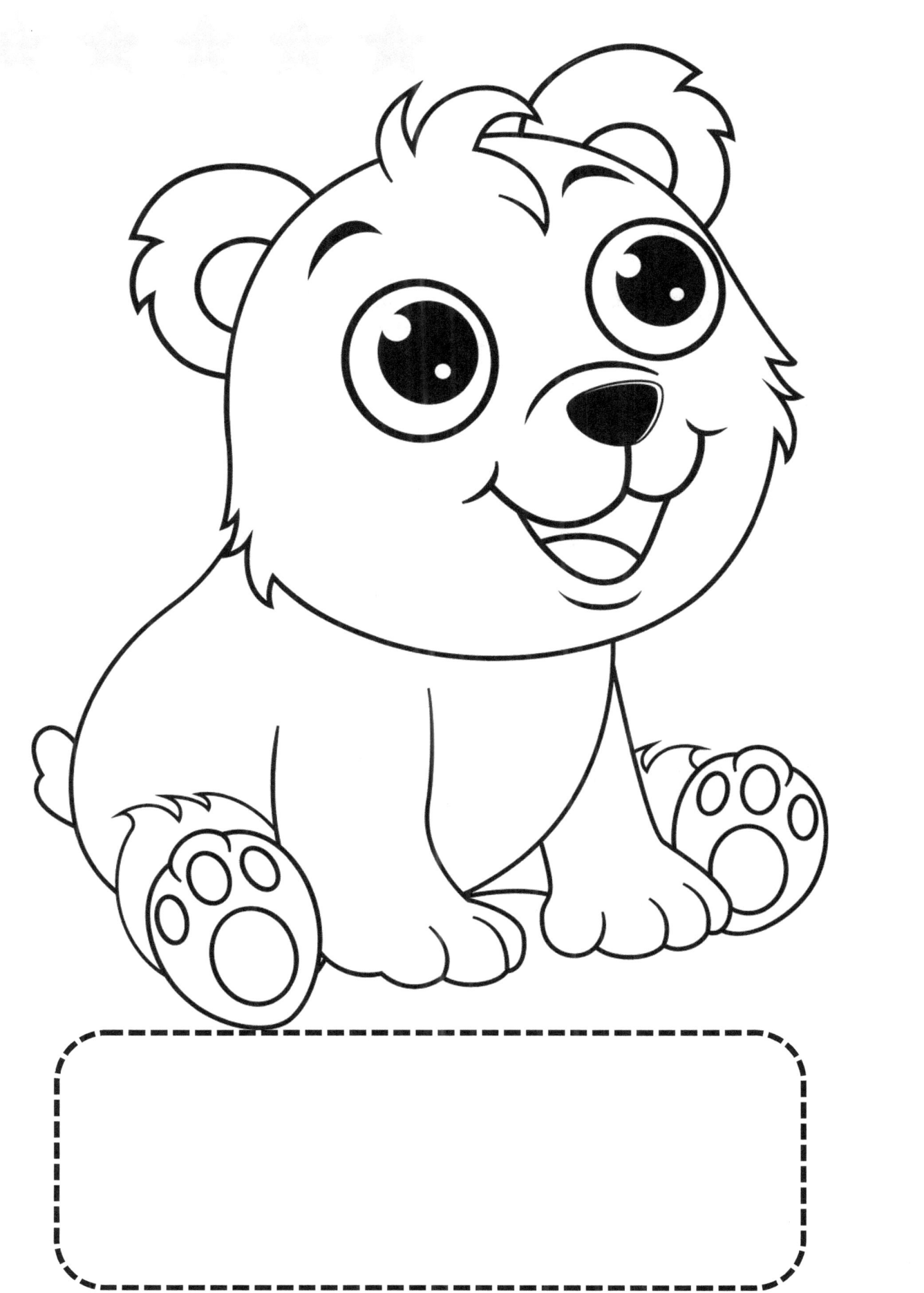

Superb!

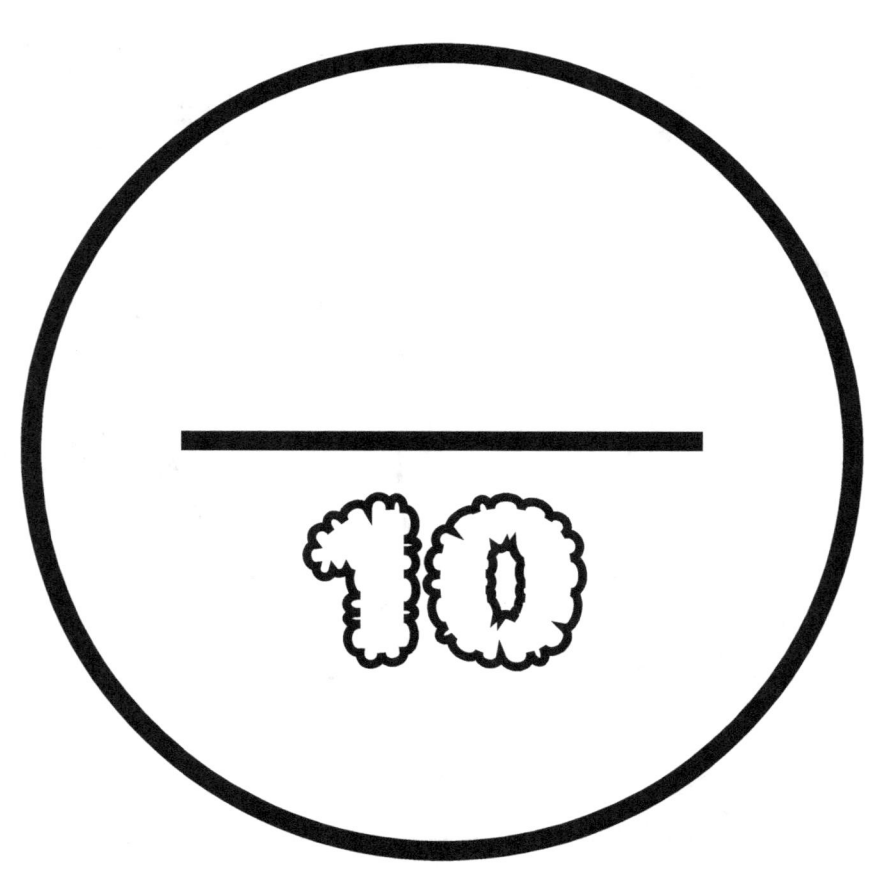

___ / 10

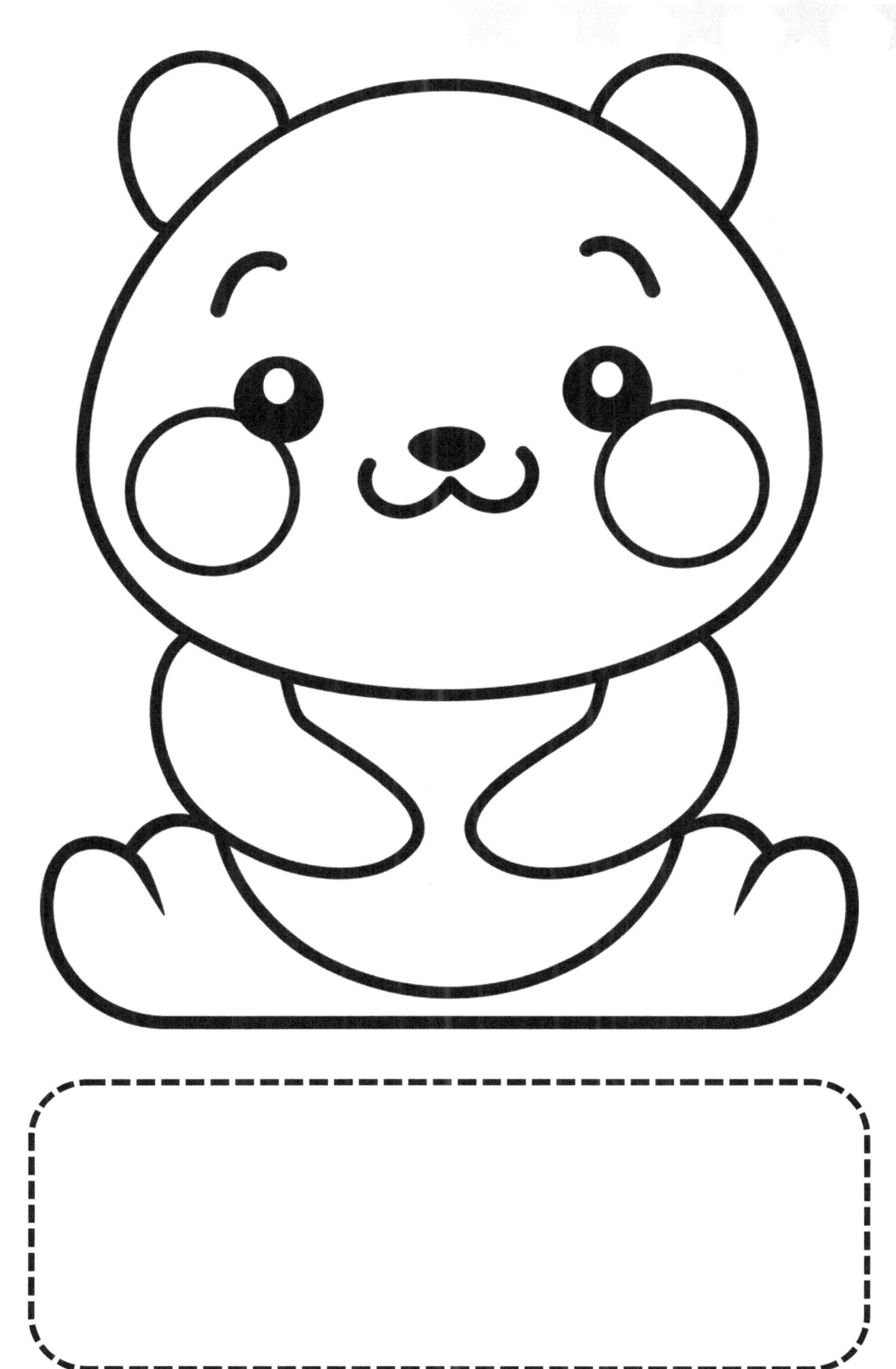

Beautifully done!

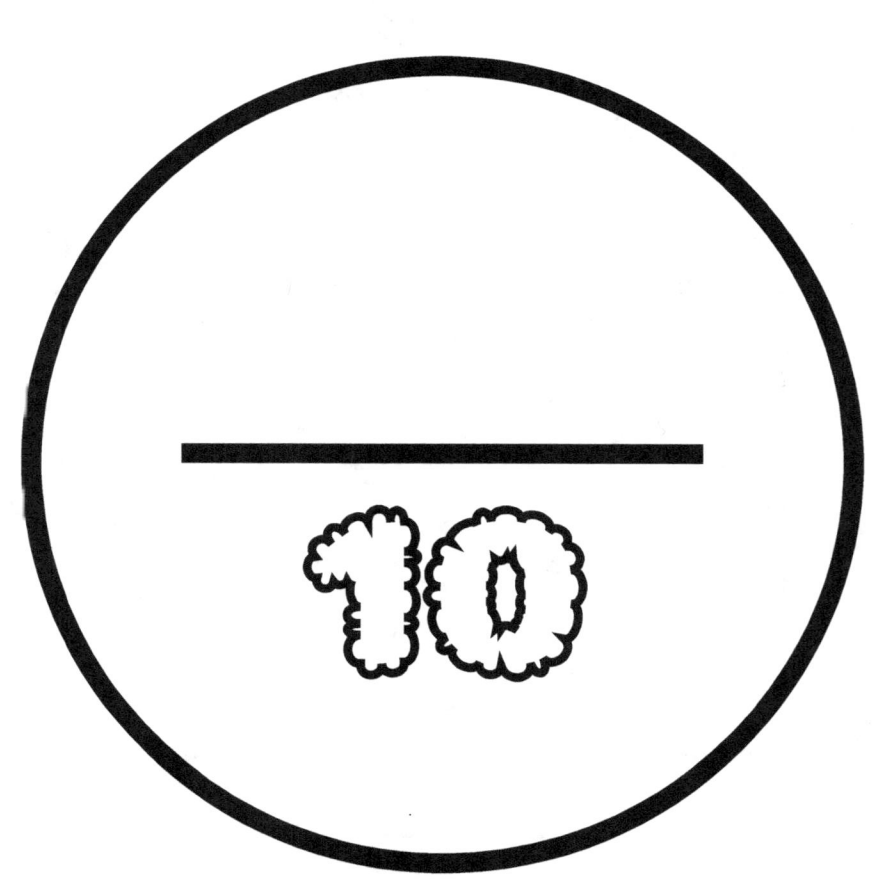

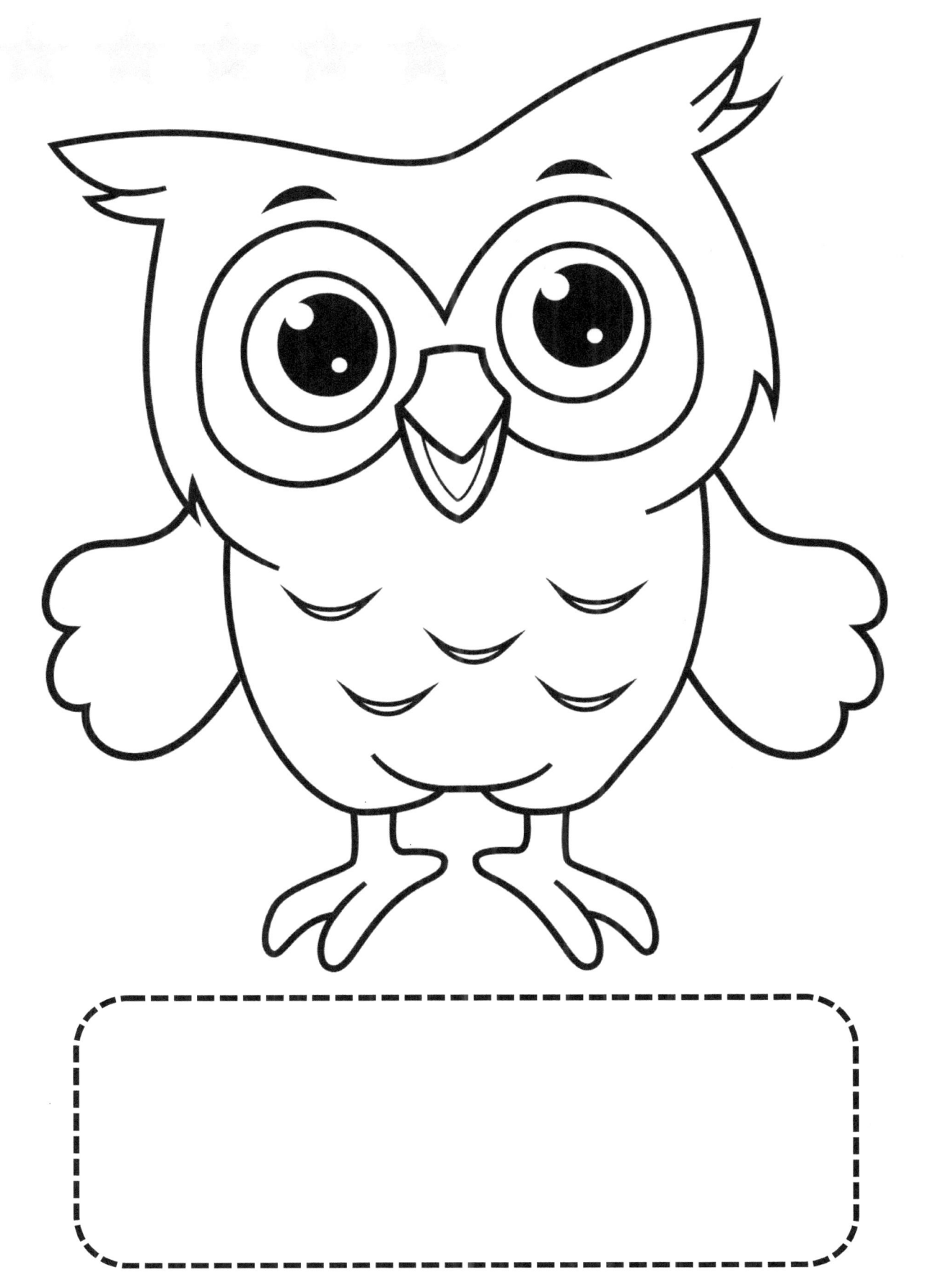

Impressive!

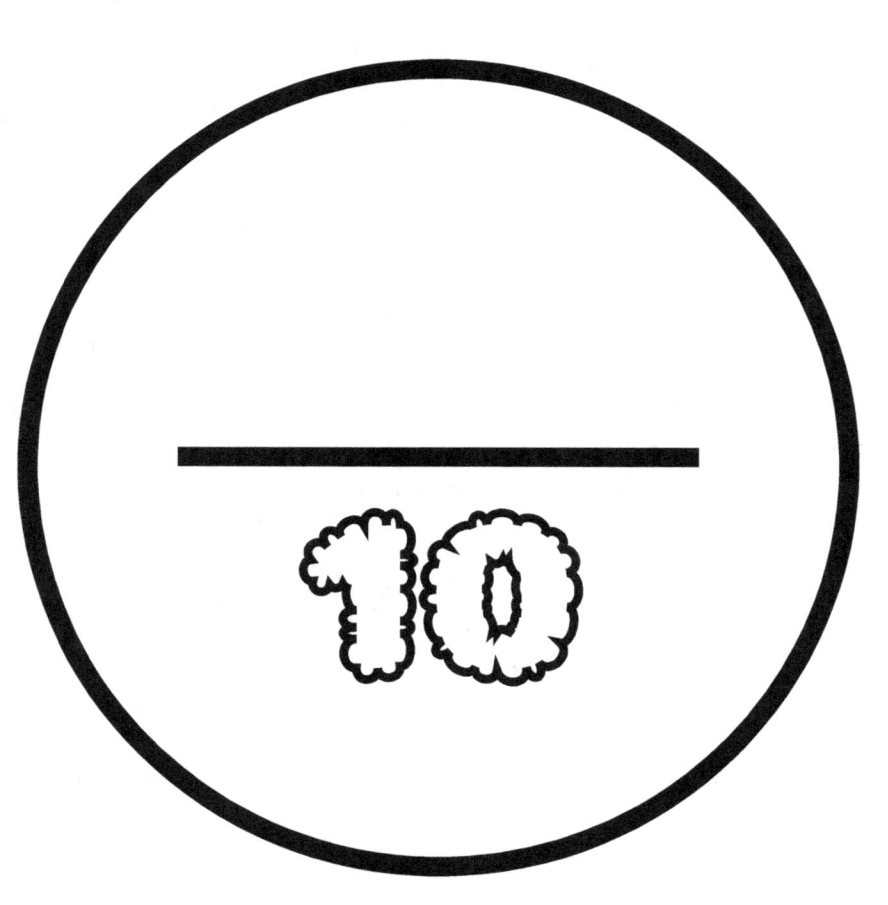

/10

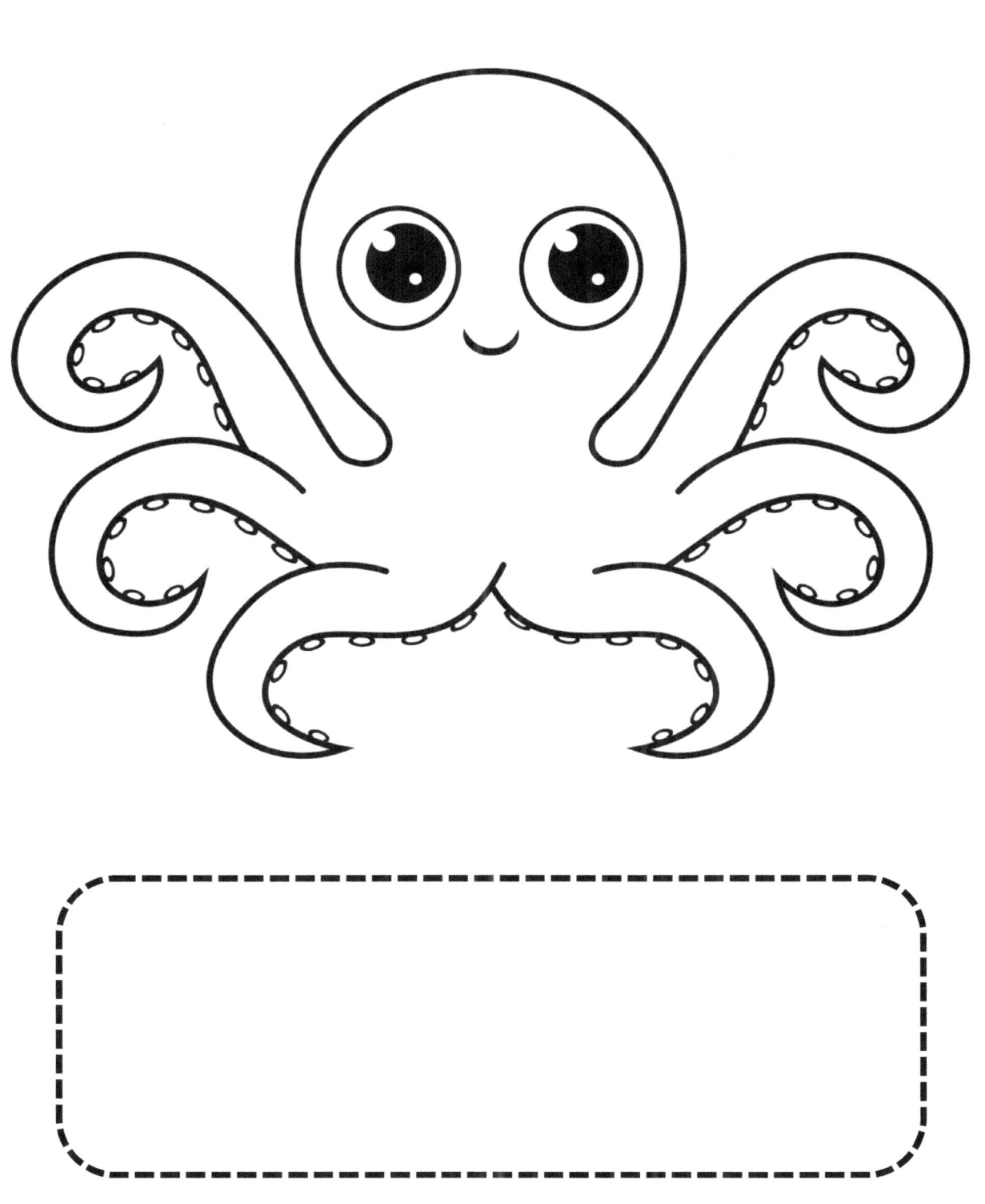

Terrific!

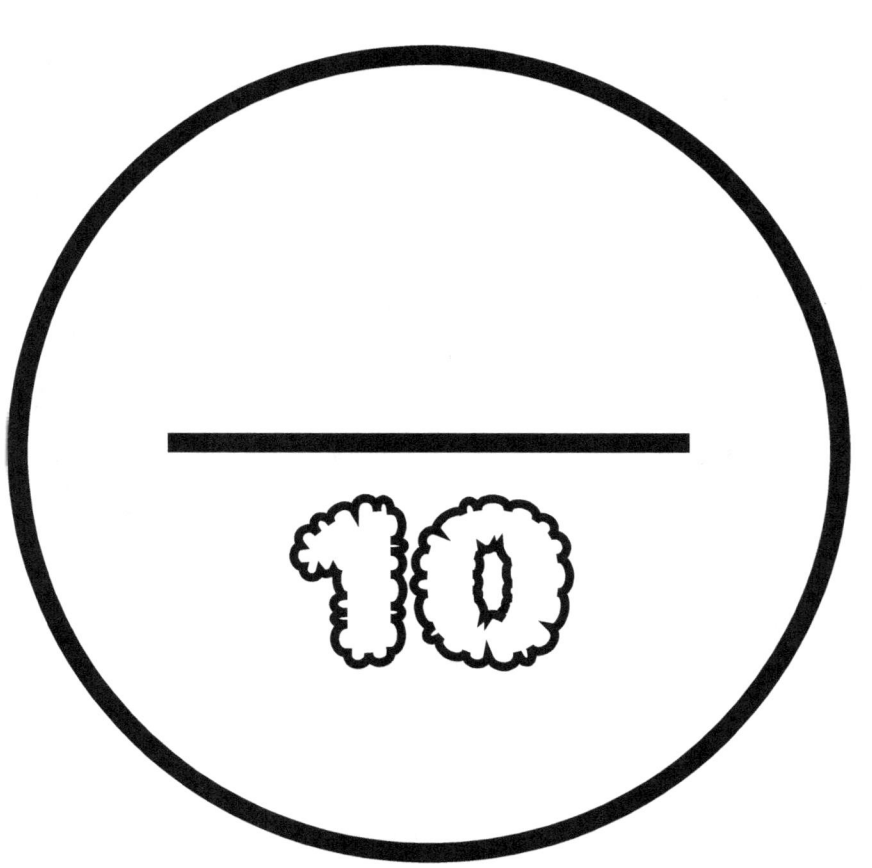

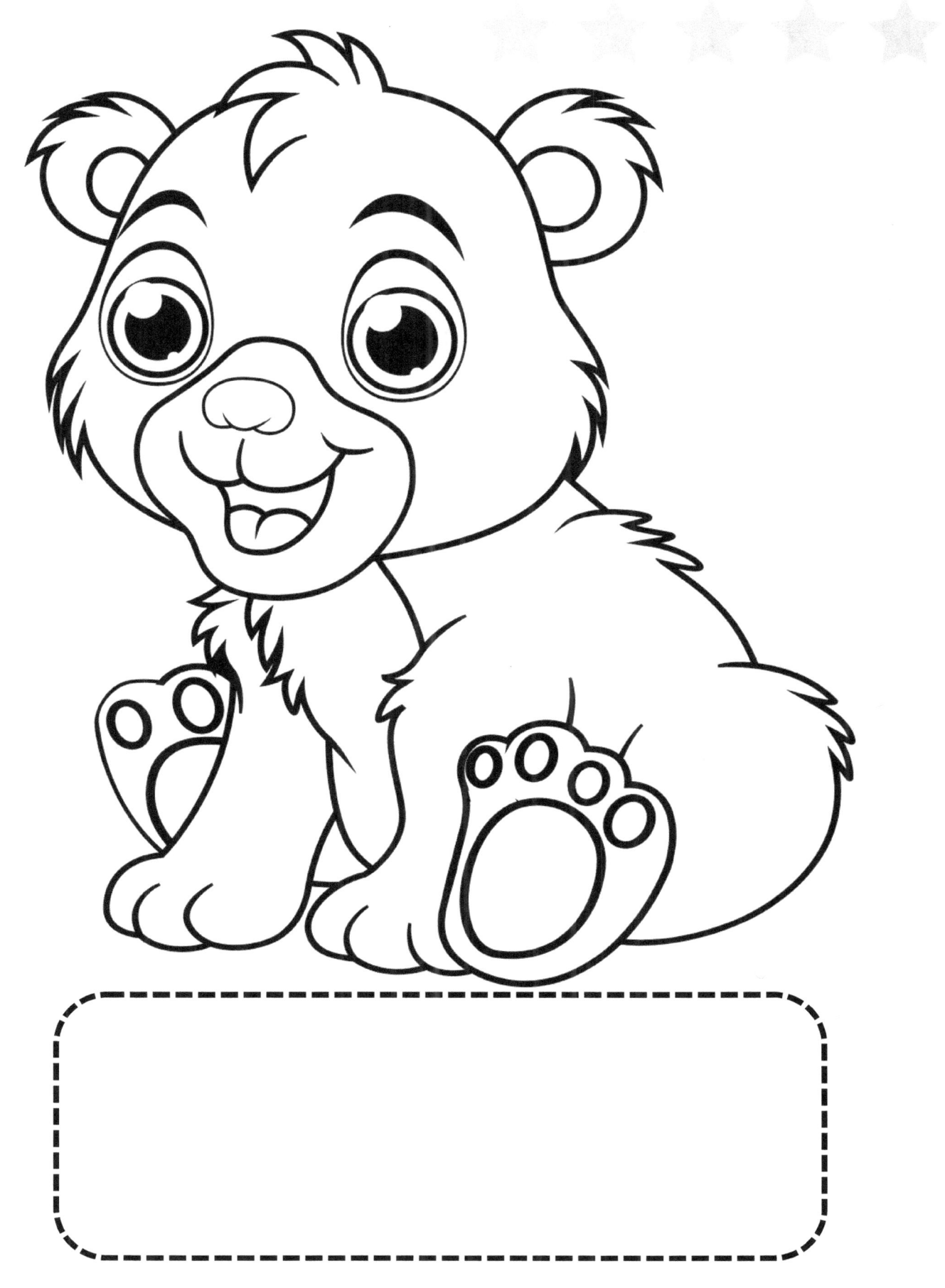

Excellent work!

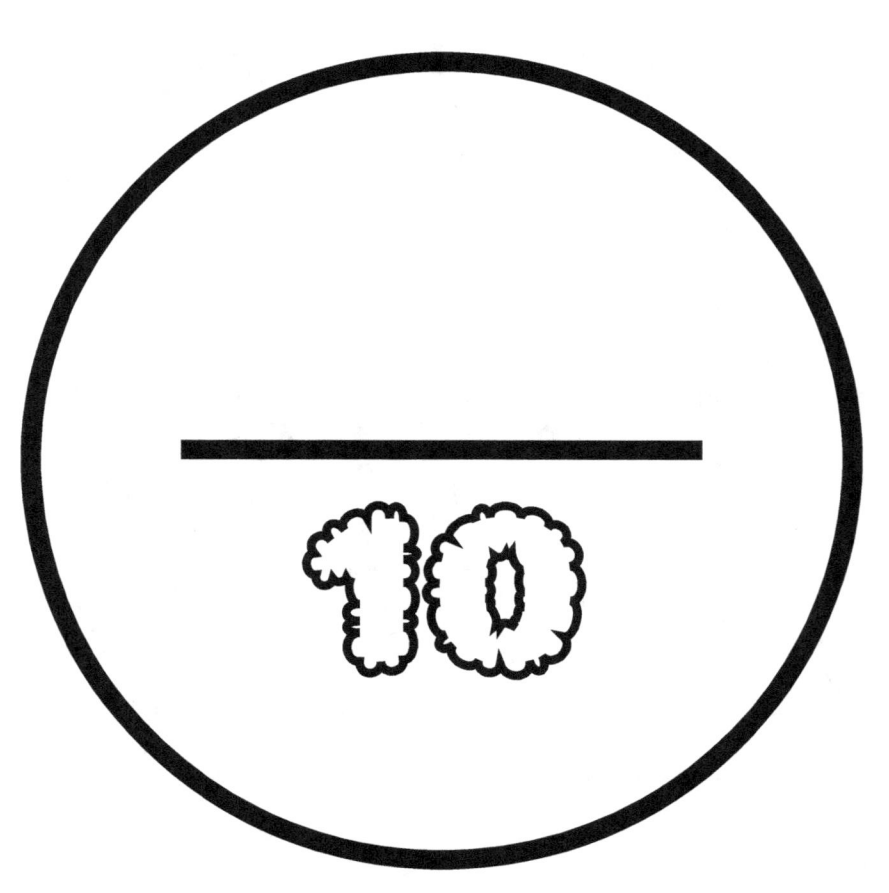

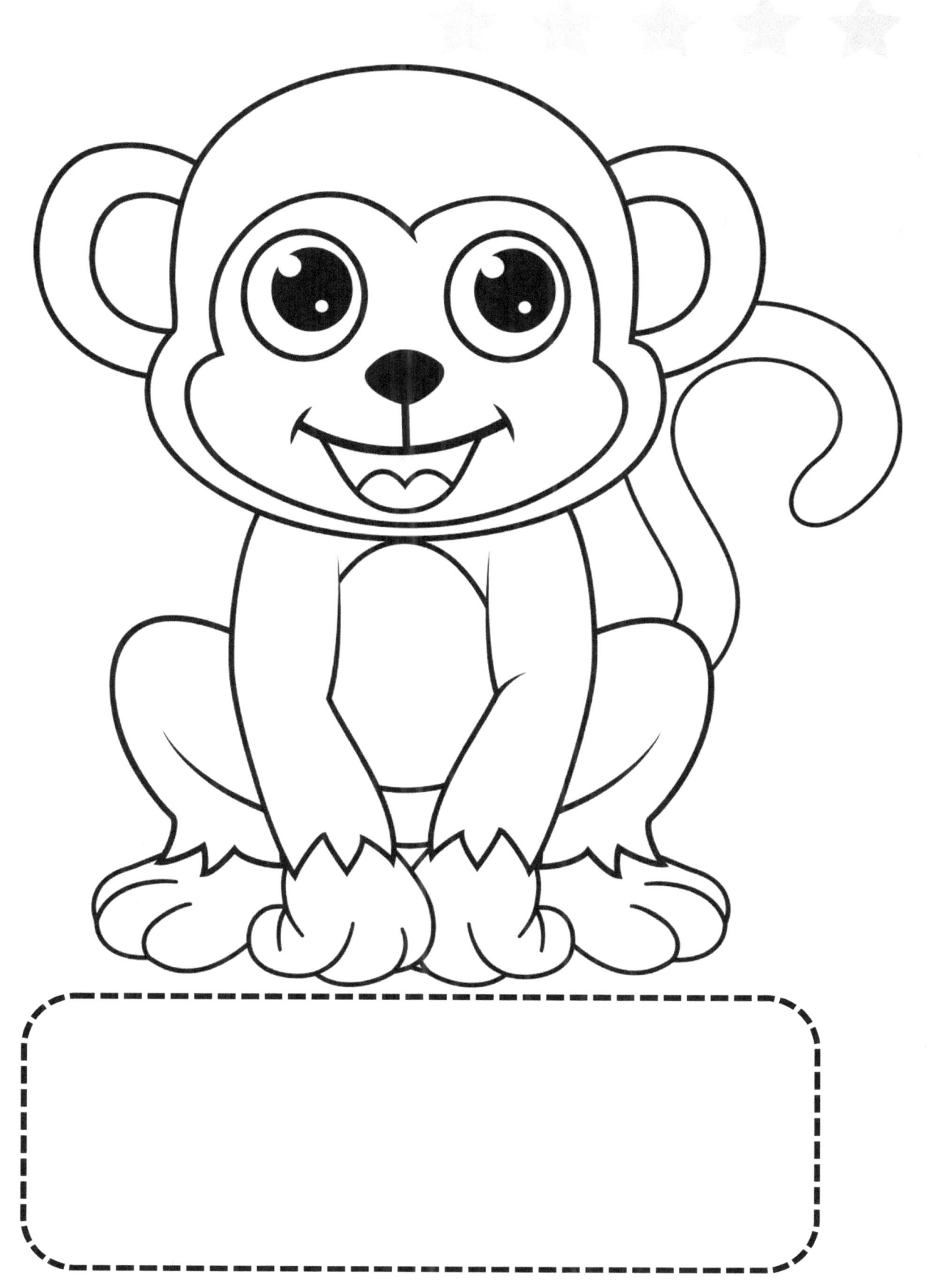

Excellent work!

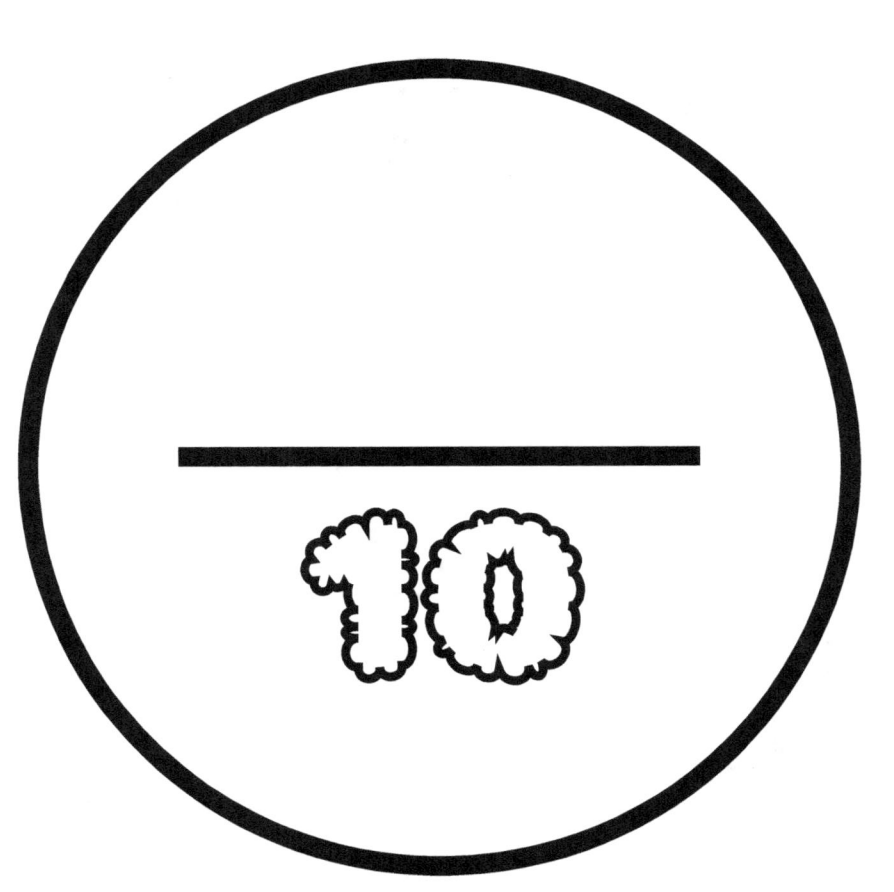

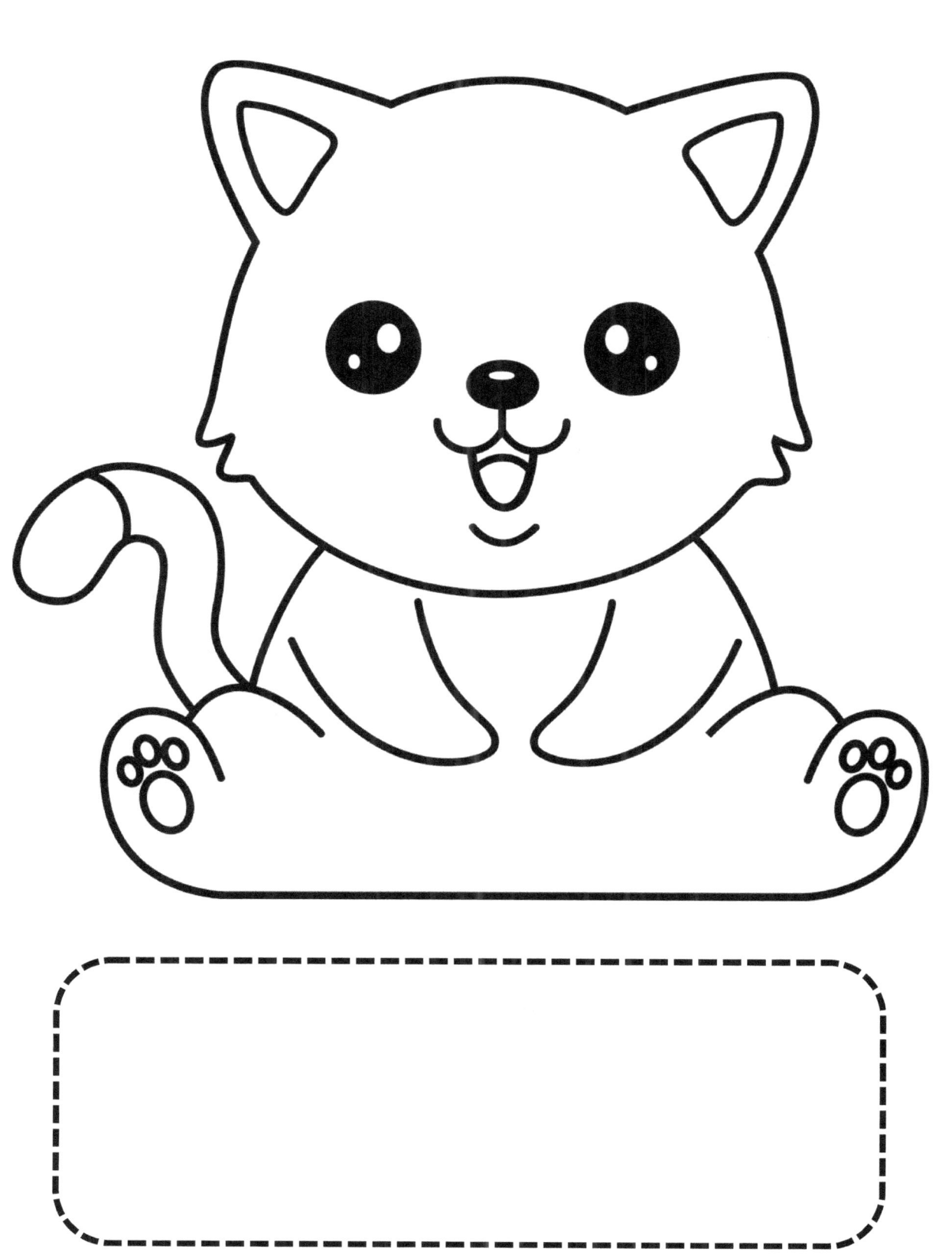

Remarkable!

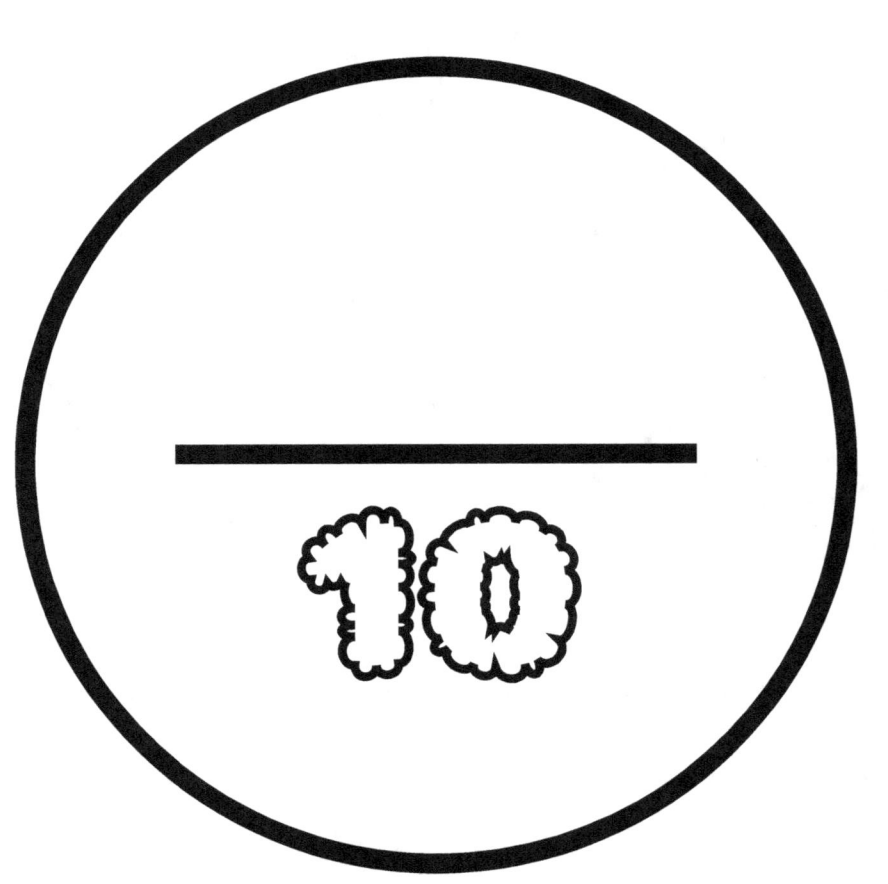

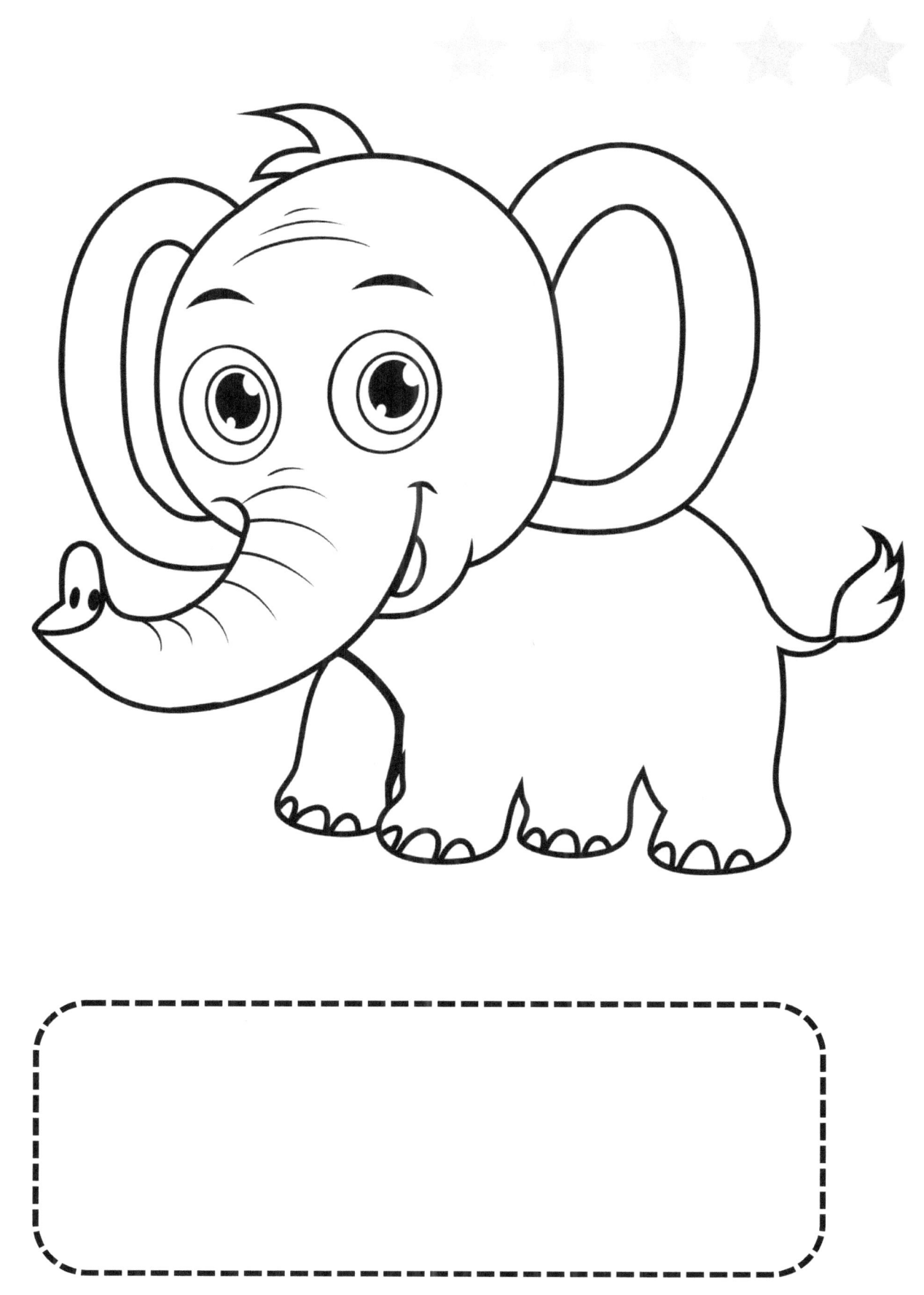

Splendid!

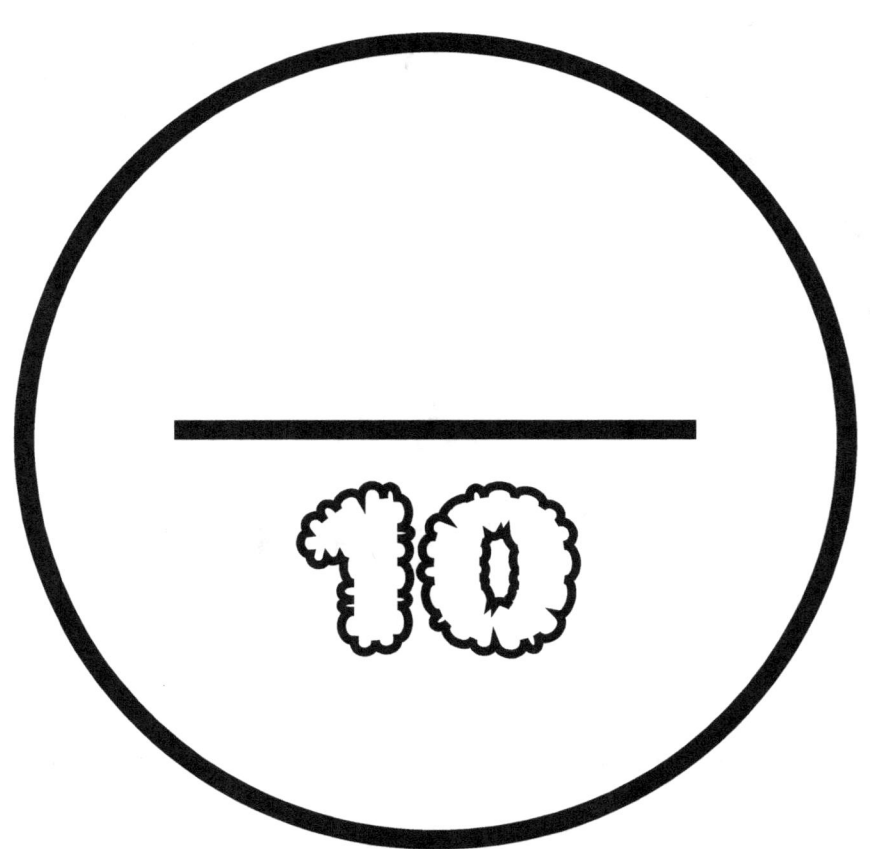

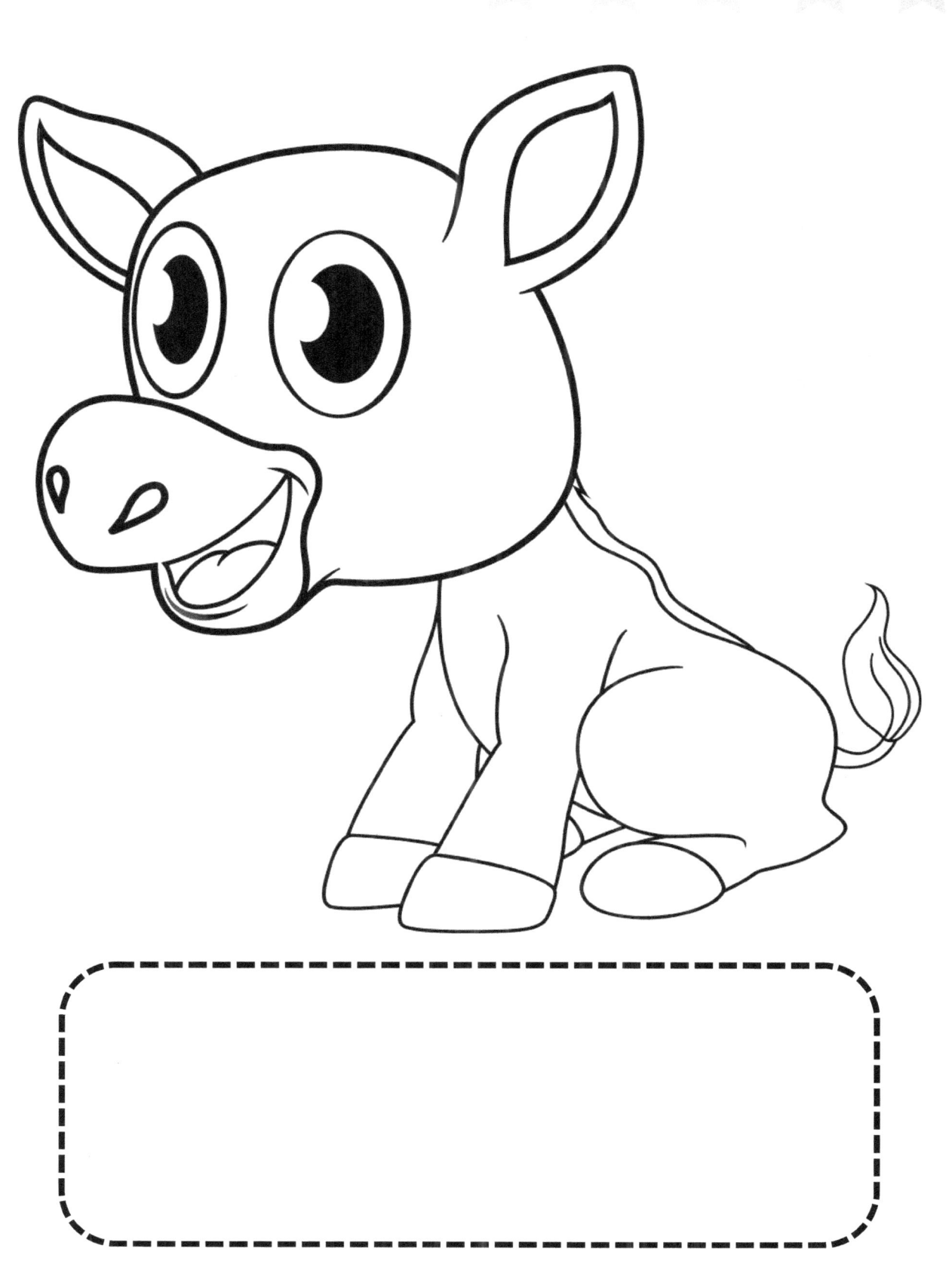

Marvelous!

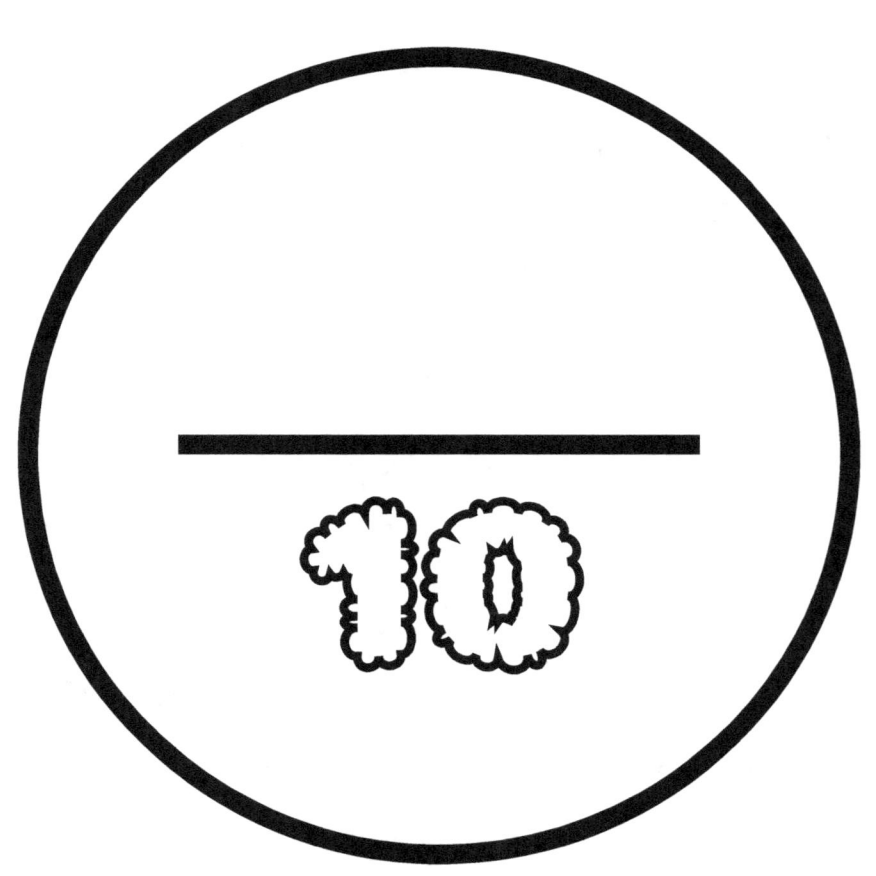

$\dfrac{\quad\quad}{10}$

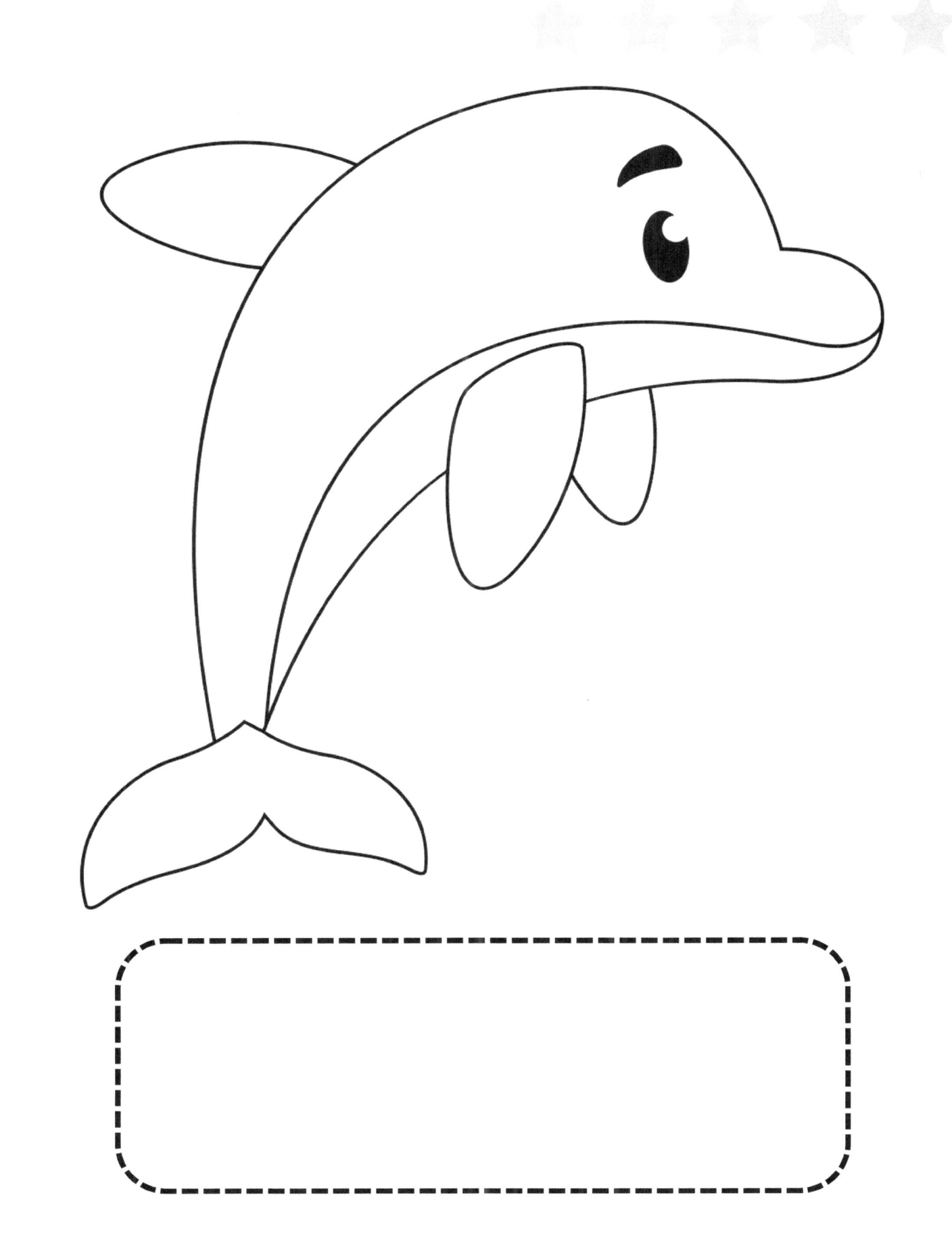

Magnificent!

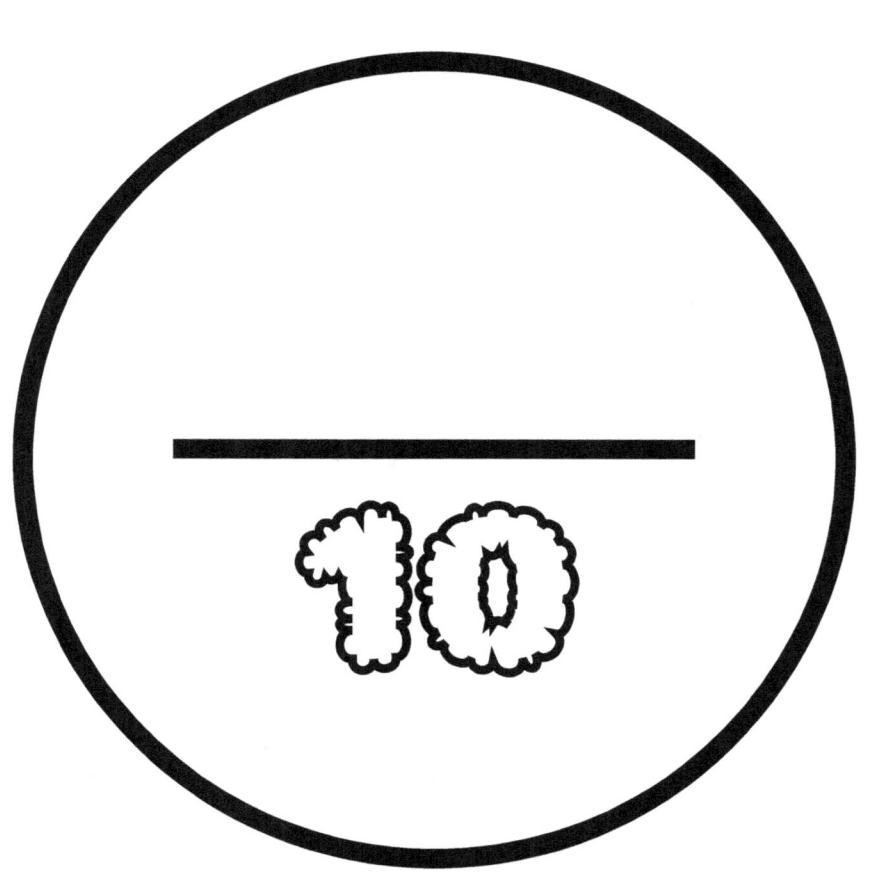

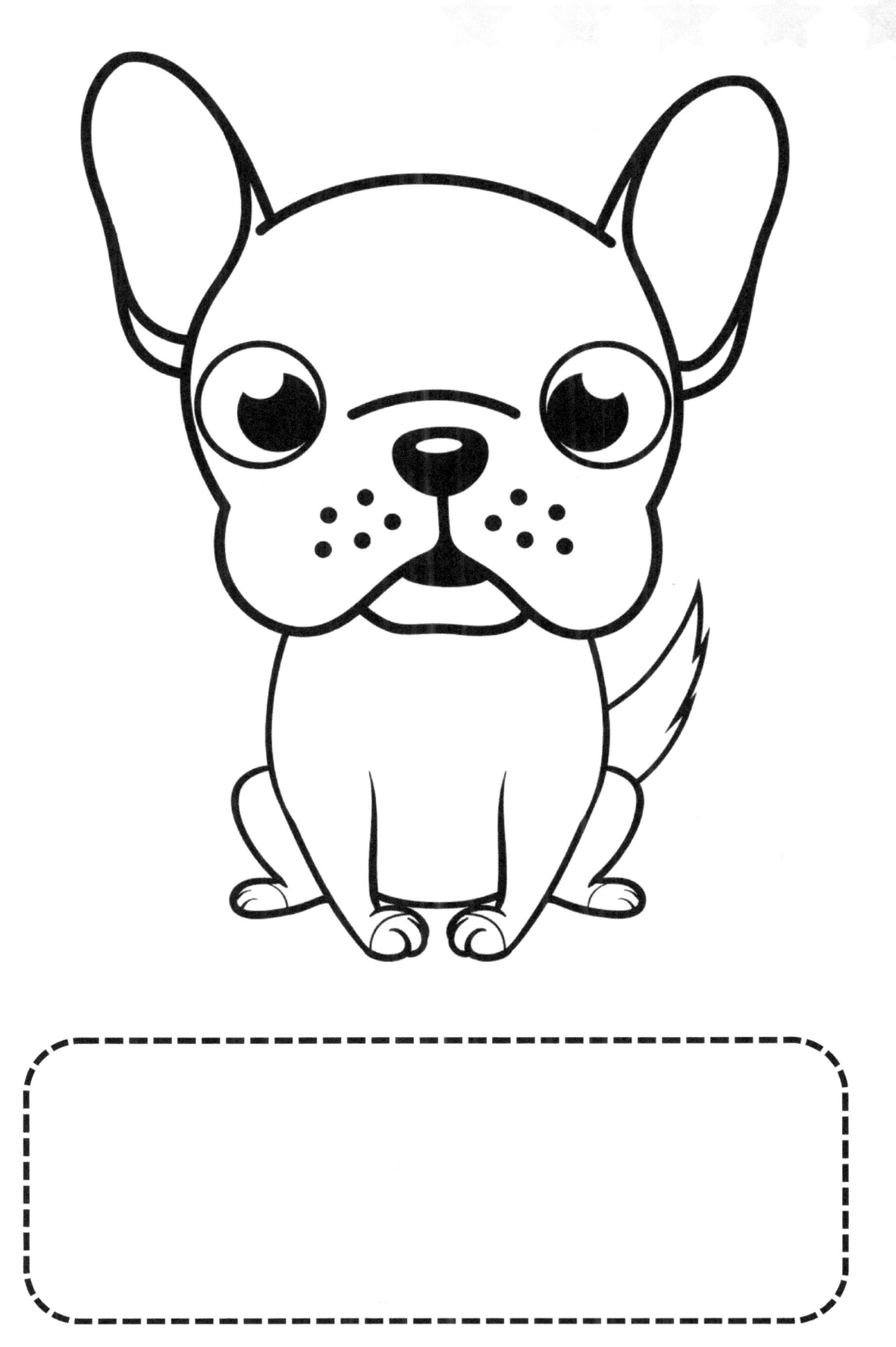

Wonderful!

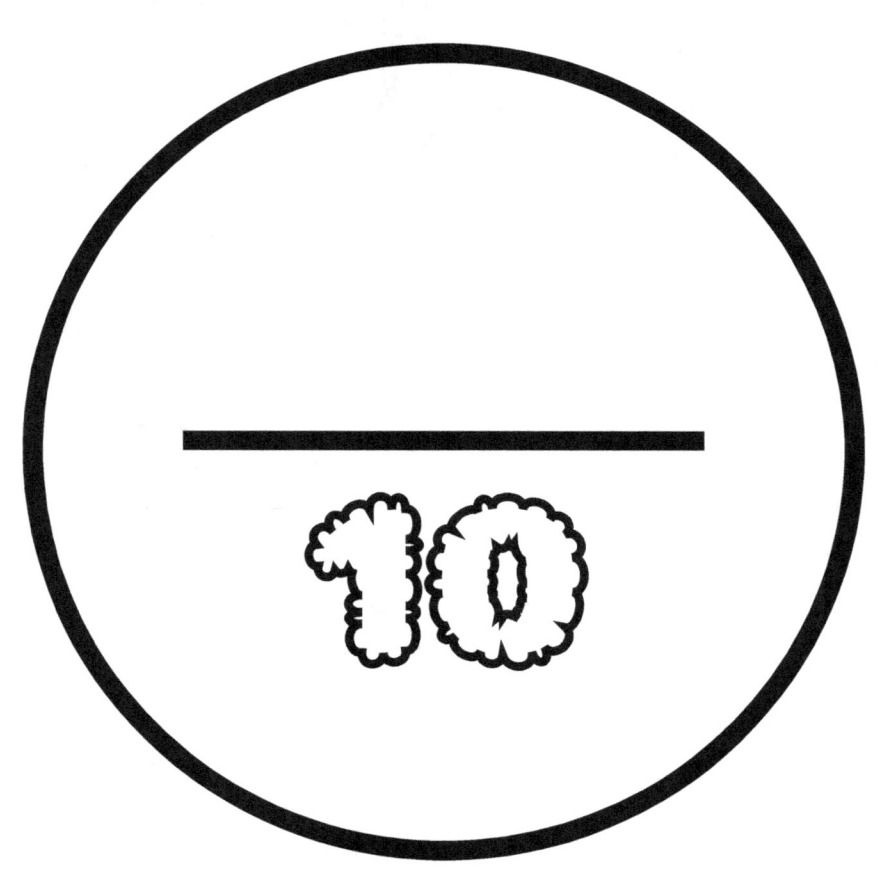

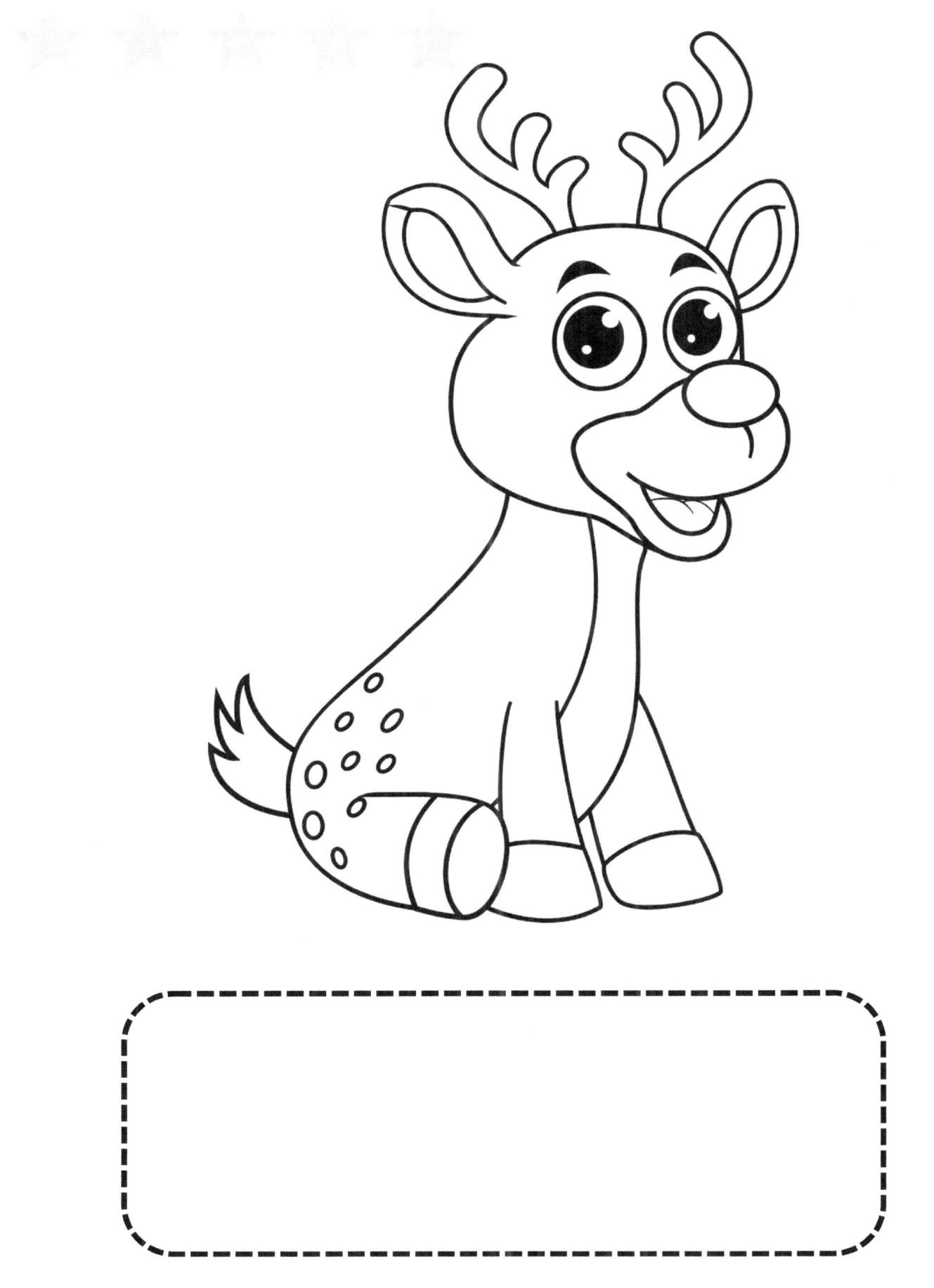

Exceptional!

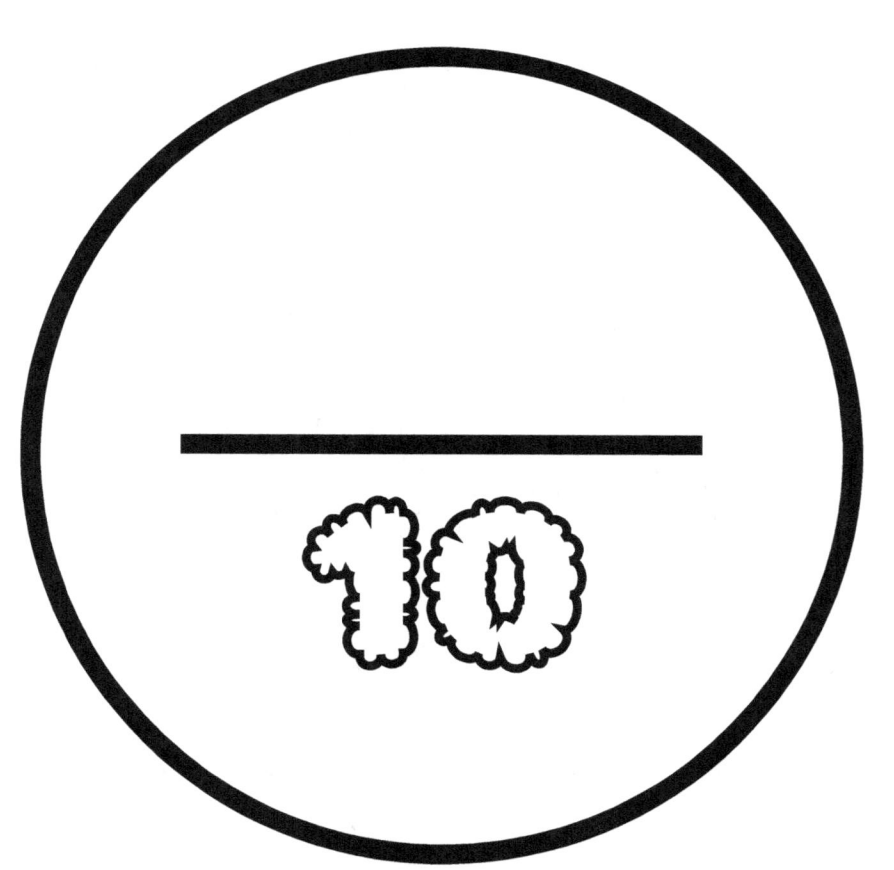

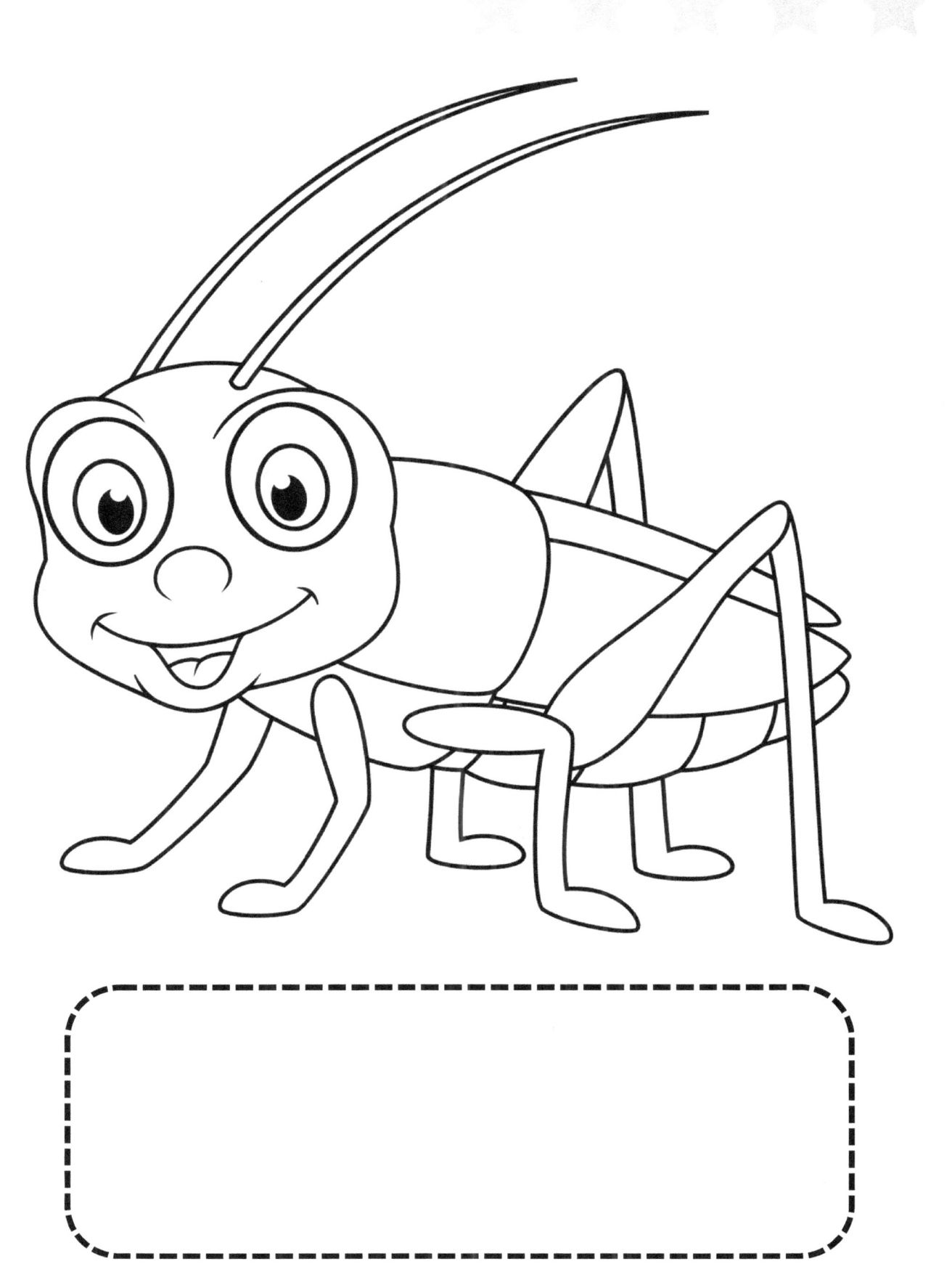

Spectacular!

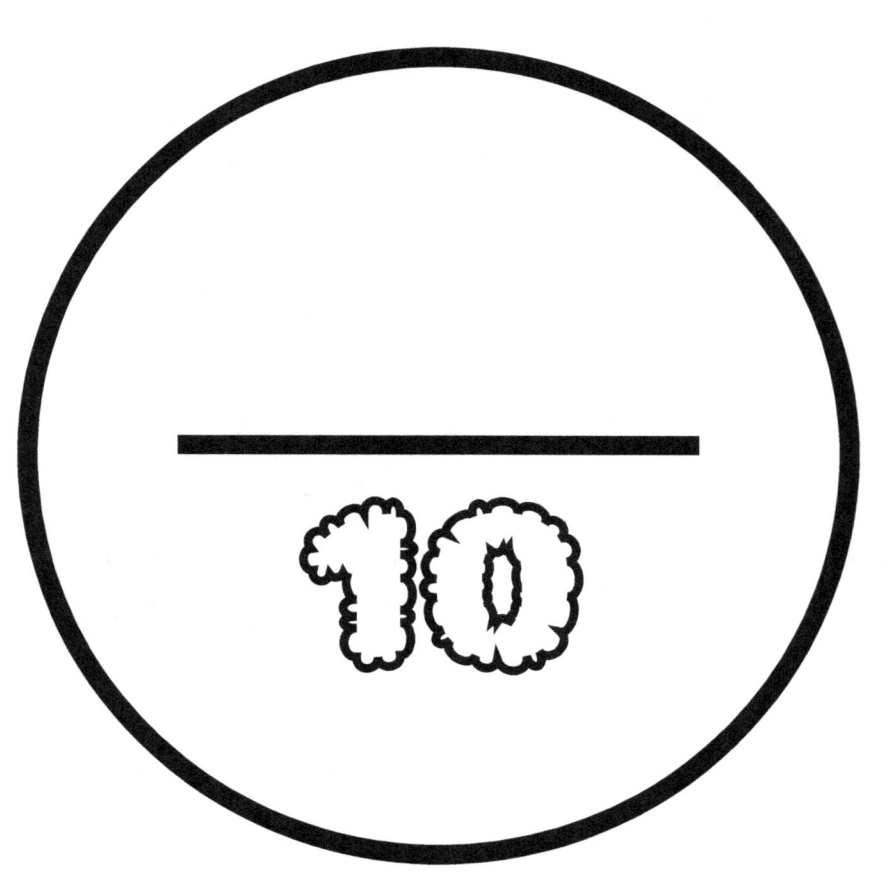

$\dfrac{}{10}$

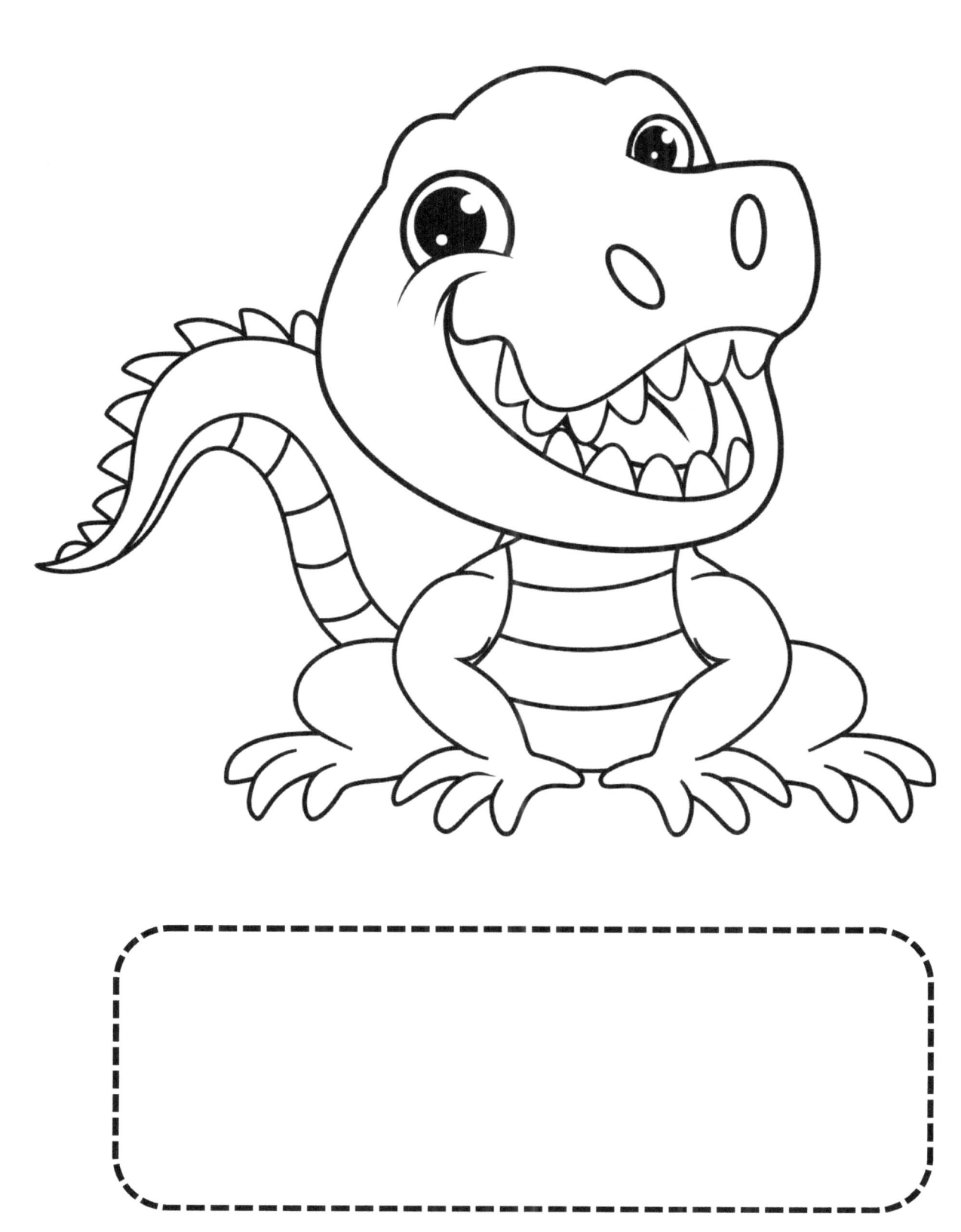

Admirable!

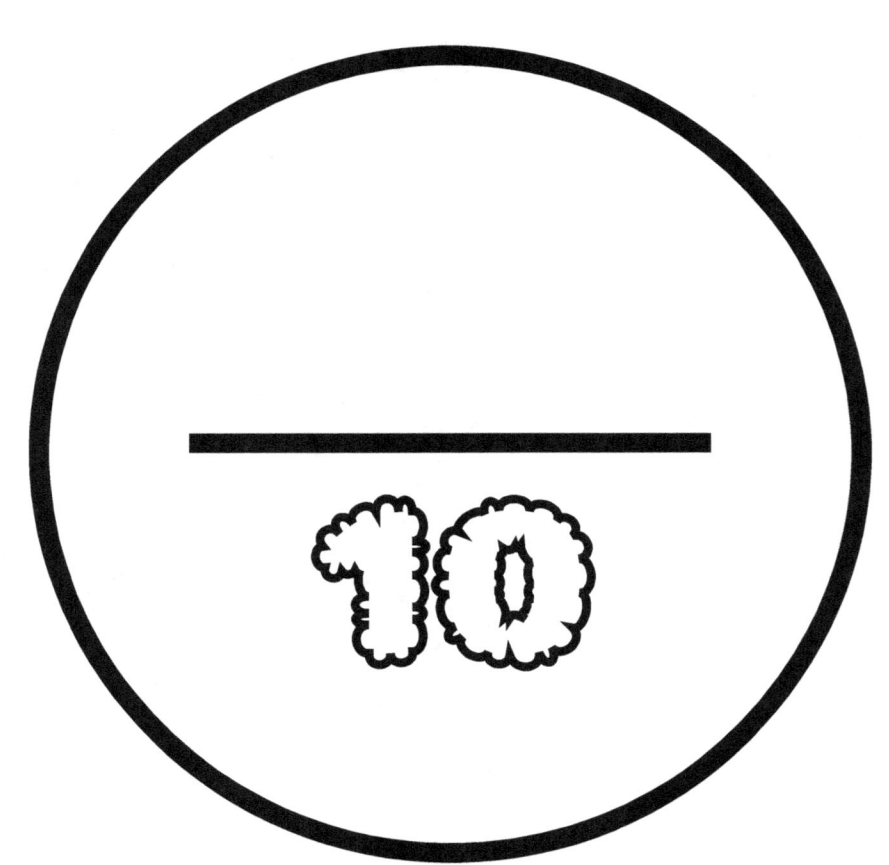

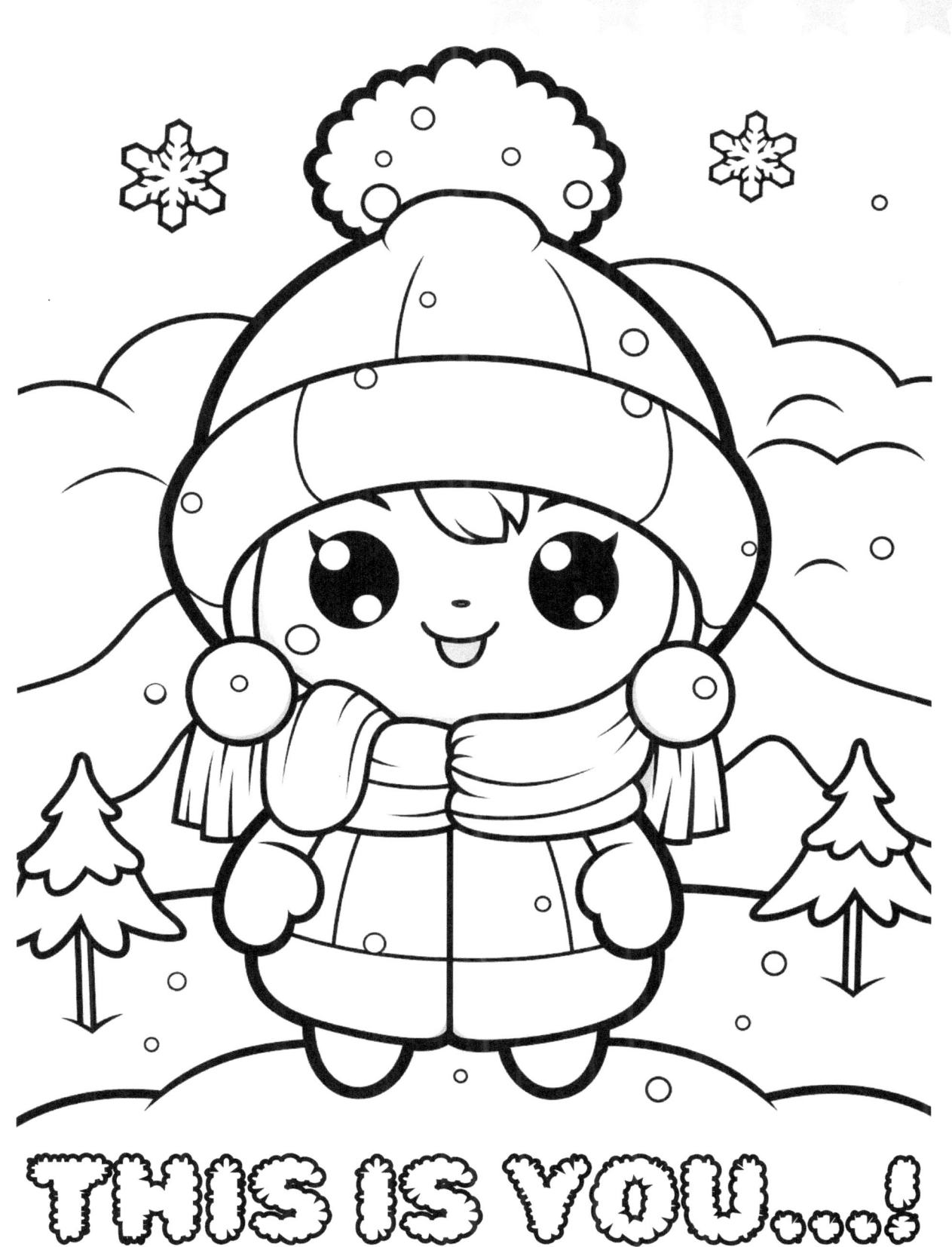

YOU'RE A TRUE ARTIST!

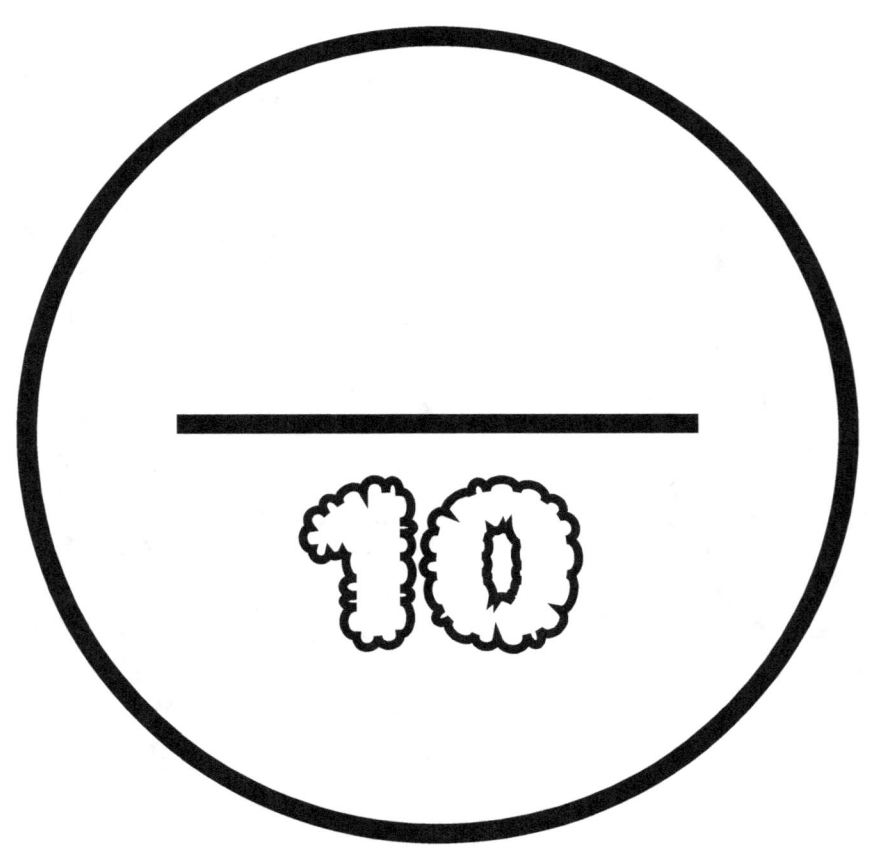

THIS IS YOU...!

www.ingramcontent.com/pod-product-compliance
Lightning Source LLC
Chambersburg PA
CBHW062206220526
45470CB00009B/2944